WILD ANIMALS OF CALIFORNIA & THE WEST
[MOUNTAINS AND DESERT: ONE]

Wild ANIMALS OF CALIFORNIA AND THE WEST

MOUNTAINS AND DESERT: ONE

by Jack Wilburn

Selected essays on the natural history of
familiar wild life of California and the western states
including all or parts of Washington, Oregon, Nevada, Wyoming,
Utah, Idaho, Montana, Arizona, New Mexico, Texas
and western Canada.

Illustrations by Tom Zanze

Cougar Books   Sacramento

© 1979 Cougar Books.
All rights reserved.
PO Box 22246, Sacramento, Ca 95822.

Drawings printed by permission of The
    Sacramento Bee.
Book Design by Jon Goodchild
Edited by Alan Pritchard
Printed in the United States of America

Library of Congress Catalog Card Number:
    76-29497
ISBN - 0-917982-05-3 (Series)
ISBN - 0-917982-12-6 (Vol. I)

To Phyllis,
my kindred spirit
on countless nature trails.

Artist Tom Zanze began drawing pictures when he was in grammar school. After attending the Academy of Advertising Art in San Francisco and putting in a stint at freelancing, he joined the Sacramento Bee art staff as a retoucher and cartoonist. Since 1972 he has been supervising artist in the newspaper's central art room.

Tom's hobbies are tennis, camping, bird watching, cooking, and collecting military antiques. He is a member of the Sierra Club, the Wildlife Federation, and the Whale Protection Fund as well as the Northern California Cartoonists and Humor Association and the Sacramento Art Directors and Artists Club.

He and his wife, Wilma, have a son and a daughter in college.

[CONTENTS]

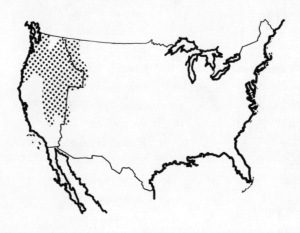

Note on Range Maps

The shaded areas on the maps show the general range of the species. These do not indicate how populous or rare a species might be. Within their overall range, a species may be found only in certain habitats with the proper combination of vegetation and physical factors. In most cases, human activities have reduced the ranges from what they formerly were.

The ranges shown for birds show only those regions where each species breeds. Migratory birds may winter long distances from their breeding ground. Some species actually fly north after breeding, before migrating south for the winter.

I ntroduction: What may seem like a minor event at the time can determine the

entire course of one's life. In analyzing the sinuous, detour-cluttered pathway of my own, I recognize such a major turning point occurred when I was eight years old.

My third grade teacher was Mrs. Revanaugh — I never learned her first name and, after the passage of 40 years, I'm not even sure I have spelled her last correctly. If she still lives she would be quite elderly, for my mental image of her at that time is of a slender, gray-haired little lady in her fifties.

What made Mrs. Revanaugh unique was her firm insistence that nature study be added to the dry three-Rs that dominated the curriculum of that pre-ecology period. In her class, nature study meant getting out of the sterile environment of that poorly lit brick building and meeting nature on its home ground. For a one-hour period twice each week, she led her troops on a nature walk into the urban wilderness of south Los Angeles.

I disliked school but I put up with it just for those two beautiful hours. Because they were the most evident of the urban wild things, birds were most often the objects of our observations. However, we didn't limit our quest to avian subjects. That sensitive lady had a name and a spell-binding story for almost every living thing we encountered. In those few cases where she didn't, when we returned we looked it up and studied the mystery creature. Mrs. Revanaugh kept her own library of nature books and field guides in the classroom, on a special shelf over her old oak desk.

To say that Mrs. Revanaugh turned me on to nature would be an understatement. I was transformed from a normal eight-year-old into a hopeless naturephile. Learning the seemingly infinite secrets of the natural world became an all-consuming passion — a passion that has intensified with the years.

The essays in this book represent gleanings from my own 40 years of observing nature throughout the West, as well as tidbits lifted from the voluminous natural history literature. It would be impossible to list all the books and periodicals I have researched in writing these columns, but the bibliography contains a list of those I most frequently used.

I have often been accused of showing an antihunting bias in my writing. That is true and I make no apologies for it. Hunting, whether for food, fur, feathers, or fun, has played a major role in the extinction of all-too-many life forms and is a factor in the threatened status of a long list of others.

Though I personally would not mourn the passing of that form of behavior called sport hunting, I must admit it has benefited wildlife in certain ways. Most importantly, revenues generated by the sale of hunting licenses and tags, and taxes on arms and ammunition have helped purchase, and thus save, critical habitat for nongame as well as game species.

I am far too much of a realist to believe that sport killing of wildlife will cease during my lifetime. There is an encouraging trend, however, that could decimate the already dwindling ranks of hunters. This is the rapidly growing sport of wildlife photography.

An ever-increasing number of Americans, many of them ex-hunters, are discovering the thrill of stalking wildlife with a camera. They realize that the trophy value of a good photograph of an animal greatly exceeds that of its mounted head.

Photography offers a greater challenge than the killing of wildlife, for it must be done at much closer range and in better light conditions. Even a mediocre shot can kill a deer at 500 yards with a modern scope-sighted rifle. To get a good frame-filling photograph of the same animal would require getting to within less than 50 yards, even using a telephoto lens.

The camera hunter enjoys year-around open seasons with no bag limits. Every form of life, regardless of size, is a potential trophy. A wary butterfly or dragonfly can be as difficult to stalk as a bobcat or fox. National parks, wildlife refuges, and other such sanctuaries off-limits to the gun toter are happy hunting grounds for the photographer and offer almost unlimited subject possibilities.

Wildlife photography is a nonconsumptive use of our wildlife resources. When the gun hunter takes a trophy, the animal is dead and never again can be enjoyed by others, regardless of the pride and joy it brings to the slayer. In contrast, any number of camera hunters can bag the same animal and its value to other users is in no way diminished when thus bagged.

Wildlife photography has been good to me. It, combined with nature writing, has given my wife, Phyllis, and me the opportunity to satisfy a long-time dream. We have become full-time naturalists — birding bums some of our friends call us.

Our home is where we choose to park our self-contained travel trailer. No longer need we drive hundreds of miles on weekends or short vacations to find new life forms to study and photograph. Now, when we find a place we especially enjoy, we can stay a day, a week, or a month — we don't have to hurry home — we are already there.

In our chosen lifestyle, our needs are simple and our wants are few. We earn our living doing the very things we would be doing if we didn't have to work at all. Our days are spent observing and photographing wildlife and plants — our evenings are spent writing about them and labeling and indexing the color transparencies we take of them. A typical work day begins at dawn and may end with a late night walk to see what the owls have to say about the events of the day.

Let me confess to another of my biases — although I profess to be a generalist in the field of nature, birds are my favorite group of animals. Phyllis and I are hopelessly caught up in the sport of bird listing and often choose the route of our travels so as to see the greatest number of new or life-list birds. This will perhaps explain the obviously disproportionate number of essays devoted to avian subjects. Because of this it was not possible to make the division of animals in this book and series by category or genetically, as I would prefer to do. So we compromised on a breakdown by regions. The difficult thing with this approach is that these choices are arbitrary. For instance, the bobcat's range is beyond the mountains, the golden eagle is a desert and grassland bird as well as in the mountains. The Pacific salmon lives most of its life in the ocean but migrates to spawn, termites are urban as well as forest dwellers, and so on.

Jack Wilburn
Nature Watching

Part One

THE
MOUNTAINS

High mountain ranges such as the Sierra Nevada, the Cascades, or the Rockies, offer a cool summer refuge for humans who live in the hot valleys below. By moving upslope with advancing spring, you can extend this most enjoyable time of the year for almost six months. In California, spring arrives on the floor of the Sacramento Valley in March but doesn't reach the tops of some Sierran peaks until August.

In traveling from valley floor to mountain top, you experience a series of life zones or vegetational belts that correspond to similar zones encountered in traveling much greater south to north horizontal distances. Each zone is characterized by its own typical plant associations and animals.

Many animals, especially birds, make seasonal upslope and downslope migrations. The Yellow-bellied Sapsucker, a woodpecker with strange food habits, nests in the high aspen groves near timberline but moves down to the foothills in fall and winter. Mule Deer also make annual upslope and downslope migrations and are followed along the way by their major predator, the Mountain Lion.

When the mountains are covered by winter's deep snow, few wild things can be found. Many that don't migrate spend the winter in hibernation. One of the champion hibernators is the Golden-mantled Squirrel, which may spend half its life sleeping away the long mountain winters. The Black Bear, which may also sleep during much of the winter, is not a true hibernator. It is a fitful sleeper and may wake up and leave its winter den during periods of mild weather.

The thick forests of the mid elevations are home to several species of owls. One of the most difficult to find is the rare and secretive Spotted Owl, which usually spends the day sleeping in a dense conifer. It will sometimes answer an imitation of its call, one version of which sounds like a barking dog. More numerous but equally as difficult to find is the tiny Saw-whet Owl, which nests in old woodpecker holes.

Another nocturnal cavity dweller is the little Northern Flying Squirrel. It doesn't really fly, but can glide amazing distances on the web of skin stretched between its extended legs. It is far more numerous than rather infrequent sightings indicate.

A fierce avian predator of the mountain forests is the Goshawk. It has short rounded wings that allow quick maneuvering when flying through the trees. Although large birds, such as Blue Grouse, are its favorite food, it also will take small mammals such as squirrels and rabbits.

The mountains of the West are home for many rare animals that have dwindled in number as human populations have exploded. One of the rarest is the Wolverine, a large relative of the weasel, famous for its great strength and bad temper. It seems to be currently holding its own and may even be increasing in number in a few areas of protected wilderness in the Sierra. Simply knowing there is a chance of seeing one of these almost mythical creatures adds excitement to hiking in the high country.

Mountain Lions are naturally shy and not a threat to humans.

1

Mystery Cat of Western Mountains: Cougar, Puma, Panther, Painter, Catamount, and Mexican Lion are just a few of the colorful local names for a great feline predator known to science as *Felis concolor*. Best known in the West as the Mountain Lion, this graceful creature was described by one team of researchers as "the mysterious American cat."

Indeed, the natural history of the Mountain Lion long has been shrouded in mystery made even more opaque by the hodgepodge of myths and old-wive's-tales that have little basis in fact.

Although several thousand Mountain Lions still roam the mountains of the West, the vast majority of human inhabitants of this region will live their entire lives without so much as a glimpse of one outside of a zoo cage. I have spent more than 30 years wandering through prime Mountain Lion habitat and have been fortunate enough to see only three of these great cats.

None of my Mountain Lion sighting was anticipated when it took place. The cats just suddenly materialized and then just as mysteriously disappeared into the mountain vastness, leaving only tracks to convince me I hadn't imagined the whole thing.

My most recent lion sighting took place on the east side of the Sierra in Mono County. It was late May and my wife, Phyllis, and I were driving to a high trailhead from which we would backpack into the beautiful and remote Silver King Basin.

We were less than a quarter mile (400 meters) from where we planned to leave our truck when a beautiful adult Mountain Lion bounded through an open patch of sagebrush and disappeared into a small grove of lodgepole pines less than a hundred yards ahead of us. We each grabbed a gunstock-mounted camera and left the truck with doors wide open in the middle of the two-rut mountain road. Phyllis approached the patch of trees from one direction and I from the other, hoping that one of us would get a picture when the cat came out.

Somehow or other our quarry gave us the slip. We didn't see it again, but we did find and photograph its tracks where it had bounded over a patch of late spring snow in the shade of the trees. I used a 4-inch (10 centimeter) pocket knife to show scale in the photograph and the great pug-mark spread a half-inch wider than the knife was long. It was a large adult male and probably weighed more than 100 pounds (45 kilograms), the largest I have ever seen.

Before Europeans arrived in the Western Hemisphere, *Felis concolor* had the largest distribution of the world's big cats. From the rain-drenched Sitka Spruce forests of coastal Southern Alaska to the high plains of Patagonia near the southern tip of South America, many racial variations of this species had evolved under a myriad of ecological conditions. Both this large range and the numbers of lions living in it have dwindled under the impact of guns, traps, poisons, and dogs. However, a surprising number still remain in the less-settled regions of this hemisphere.

The Mountain Lion is a large and powerful predator capable of killing such formidable prey as an adult bull elk. The deer is its most important prey species and it has been estimated it takes 50 deer a year to support a single adult lion. Like most predators, lions are opportunists that will take almost any available prey. They are not above such tidbits as mice, squirrels, gophers, and birds. Many become highly successful at preying on porcupines.

Because of its great appetite for red meat, a single lion requires a large home range. A study conducted in a primitive area in Idaho, where lions fed on deer, elk, and mountain sheep, revealed one lion for each 13 square miles (34 square kilometers) of habitat. A more recent study done in the coastal mountains of California showed a lion population of about 16 to 20 animals for the 175-square-mile (450-square-kilometer) study area. Ranges of individuals were found to overlap and no lion held sway over an exclusive domain.

Female Mountain Lions give birth to litters of one to five kittens in seclusion. Like all cats, they are polygamous and the males are not involved in raising the young. There is good evidence that a male lion will dine on his own offspring if he finds them unguarded by the female.

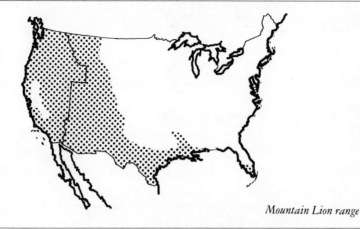

Mountain Lion range

Mountain Lion kittens are about a foot long and weigh about a pound at birth. They are blind and have black spots on their fawn-colored coats. Birth may take place in almost any month of the year, but most are born in summer.

Young Mountain Lions learn to hunt big game for themselves by the time they are about a year old, but often remain with their mother until their hunting techniques are perfected. They lose their spots when 10 months of age and from that time on are difficult to tell from their mother except by their smaller size and awkwardness.

Their appetite for venison and their occasional killing of domestic livestock have brought Mountain Lions into direct conflict with humans. They are most often hunted with hounds that trail by scent until the lion is treed or brought to bay. While a lion is more than a match for any dog, they readily tree when pursued by almost any dog that barks.

The status of the Mountain Lion slowly has been changing from that of bountied predator to game animal or even protected species in some states. In California, the controversial bounty was removed in 1963 and the animal was protected by a moratorium on hunting in 1971 — a moratorium still in effect. The lion has not fared as well in other Western states such as Arizona, where killing was still unregulated in 1979.

Mountain Lions are not considered a threat to human safety. They are shy and retiring in nature and almost never attack humans unless cornered with no other means of escape. There has been only one verified case of a human death caused by a lion in California since 1900. This involved a cat believed to have been rabid.

*In early morning sunlight, the Golden Eagle gleams
like a cascade of brilliant gold.*

2

T he Wandering Golden Eagle: It's
difficult to imagine a bird more majestic
than the Golden Eagle, *Aquila chrysaetos*. Soaring on broad wings that may
span seven feet and sporting raptorial talons as big as a man's hand, these
mighty feathered hunters are capable of taking prey many times as heavy as
themselves.

Despite its ample qualifications, the Golden Eagle lost out to its
cousin, the Bald Eagle, in the selection of our national emblem. The main
reason, I surmise, was the fact that the Golden offers allegiance to no one
nation, but wanders over the length and breadth of three continents in the
Northern Hemisphere. Here in North America, it is found from Central
Mexico to Northern Alaska and east to Newfoundland but is entirely
missing as a breeding bird in the Eastern United States.

In the West, Golden Eagles are far more common than their
endangered white-headed relatives. They are most at home in the high
mountains or rolling foothills, but it is not unusual to sight their
distinctive silhouettes far out over the valleys, especially during winter.

Although they appear similar in many respects, Golden and Bald
Eagles diverged from a common ancestor millions of years ago. The Golden
Eagle has been placed in the genus *Aquila*, a group of raptors that are
collectively called the true eagles. Bald Eagles were placed in *Haliaeetus*,
the fish eagles. Balds usually nest and hunt near large lakes, rivers, or
along the seacoast. Goldens have no special affinity for water and are
common in the dry sagebrush deserts of the West.

From a distance, adult Golden Eagles appear to be all black, but in good light and at close range one can see they are really brown. Their common name comes from the light tan tips of their hackles, the pointed feathers of head and neck, which gleam like a cascade of brilliant gold in early morning sunlight. The lower legs of Golden Eagles are feathered to their feet, while those of the bald are bare.

Neither Bald nor Golden Eagles obtain adult plumages until at least the fourth year of life and, until that time, have a series of juvenile and immature patterns that make identification more difficult. Young Goldens show a large patch of white on the base of the tail, as well as white windows in their wings. In young Balds, the wings show various amounts of white near the leading edges, but the white head and tail of the adult are lacking. Before the long-overdue legal protection was extended to the Goldens, many young Balds were shot by hunters who thought they were killing Goldens.

Unlike Bald Eagles, which are almost entirely tree-top nesters, Goldens prefer to place their large stick nests on a cliff-face ledge. However, where suitable cliff nest sites are lacking, Goldens also will use tall trees for their aeries.

Eagles mate for life and will return year after year to a favorite nest site if not unduly disturbed. If one member of a pair dies, the surviving spouse will bring a new mate to the old aeries the following nesting season. In this way, eagle aeries have been occupied continuously for scores of years and the nests often reach fantastic proportions as new material is added each season.

The typical clutch size for the Golden Eagle is two eggs but one, three, or rarely, four are also found. The female begins incubating as soon as she lays the first egg so the chicks hatch several days apart. She alone sits on the eggs for the 35 days of incubation, but her doting mate feeds her on the nest and stands guard to drive off intruders.

When the chicks are small, the male does most of the hunting for the family, but later both members of the pair must forage to satisfy the big appetites of the rapidly growing eaglets.

Its large size, great speed, and flying agility have made the Golden Eagle a favorite of falconers for hundreds of years. During the heyday of falconry in medieval Europe, only kings were allowed to fly eagles and any person of lesser rank caught with one on his gloved fist was made to pay with his life.

Halfway around the world, in Tartary and Mongolia, Goldens are still used to hunt wolves, just as they were in the days of Genghis Khan. They

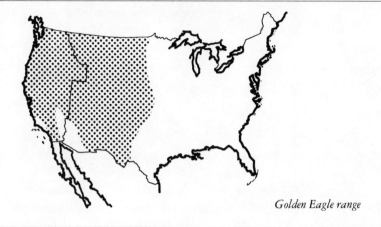

Golden Eagle range

have been used to kill prey animals as large as antelopes in parts of the world where falconry is or was practiced.

One oft-debated topic of Golden Eagle natural history is how much weight they can fly with. Even experts disagree on their load limit. I can find no authenticated reports of their carrying anything heavier than a seven-pound (3.2-kilogram) jackrabbit. One observer did report finding the carcass of a Bobcat in a Golden's nest, but the report made no mention of the age or weight of the cat.

The considerable literature on the Golden Eagle contains many accounts of their killing animals as large as adult deer and Pronghorns, so there is little doubt this is within their capabilities. These unusual attacks have mostly involved conditions such as deep snow or prey animals weakened by starvation. As are most predators, eagles are opportunists and will accept an easy meal whenever given the chance.

The main prey species for the Golden Eagle over much of the arid West is the very numerous Black-tailed Jackrabbit. Ground squirrels, Prairie Dogs, Marmots, and other rodents are eaten in large numbers and even birds are captured by these swift hunters. The lambs of domestic sheep also are taken, but certainly not to an extent to justify the war of extermination sheepmen have waged against this valuable species.

Concern for the endangered spotted cats of the world
may be threatening our own Bobcat.

3

The Stubby Tailed Cat: The Bobcat, *Lynx rufus*, is the smallest and most numerous of native wild cats that still roam the American West. Its much smaller size, spotted pelage (hair covering), and short stub of a tail make it easy to tell apart from the more rarely seen Mountain Lion. The Canadian Lynx, *Lynx canadensis*, a slightly larger relative of the Bobcat, has longer legs and more pronounced ear tufts. The ranges of the Bobcat and Lynx overlap in southern Canada and in several of our northern states.

The ubiquitous Bobcat can be found in every type of habitat in the West except areas that have been greatly modified by human activities. It occurs from below sea level in the scorching desert of Death Valley to the stunted subalpine forests of the Sierra, Cascades, and Rockies. It is most numerous in the steep canyon country at mid elevations, where rocky outcrops amid thick chaparral provide it with ideal hunting and denning.

Bobcats are larger and longer legged than domestic house cats. Adult Bobs range in weight from about 15 to 30 pounds (7 to 14 kilograms) with males somewhat larger than females. Their ears are tufted and black with a large, contrasting white spot on the back side. The absurdly short tail has a black tip and a series of black bars along the upper surface. Their beautiful coat of fur ranges from various shades of brown or gray on the back and sides to almost pure white on the belly. A heavy sprinkling of darker spots, mostly along the sides, and nattily-striped mutton-chop cheek whiskers give a final touch that makes the Bobcat one of the most beautiful of the felines.

23

Melanism, a black color phase relatively common in leopards and jaguars, is very rare in Bobcats. I had the extremely good fortune to see a melanistic Bobcat years ago in the Santa Monica Mountains of Southern California. I unknowingly walked to within 20 feet (6 meters) of where this lovely animal lay in a daytime bed in rather open chaparral. When it suddenly got up and looked me over before bounding off I could hardly believe what I was seeing. It was not solid black, but had black spots on a dark slate-gray background (look closely at a melanistic leopard and you can also see its spots).

I wasn't carrying a camera when I encountered that beautiful black Bobcat. Ever since, I have hoped for a repeat performance. There is, however, little chance of my being that lucky again. Even glimpsing a normal-colored Bobcat in the wild is a rare experience and melanism occurs in less than one Bobcat in 10,000.

Except for the brief mating season, Bobcats are solitary animals that roam over a hunting territory covering several square kilometers. When the females are in heat in late January or February, these cats may congregate in small groups and caterwaul like overgrown housecats. Anyone lucky enough to hear these unworldly shrieks and wails in the still of a winter's night is guaranteed to have the hair raise straight up on the back of their neck. I have heard caterwauling Bobcats only twice and would rate this as one of the wildest of nature's night sounds. I feel certain that many of the reports of Mountain Lions screaming in the night are actually the mating sounds of Bobcats.

About 50 days after mating, the female will give birth to a litter of one to four spotted kittens. Her nursery may be a rocky ledge or crevice on a cliff face, a hollow log, or an underground den previously dug by Coyote or Badger.

Like domestic kittens, Bobcats are born with eyes sealed shut. They grow rapidly and are weaned by early summer. The kittens remain with the mother and receive hunting instructions until early fall. Siblings often remain together through their first winter and then split to become solitary hunters.

Like all members of the cat family, Bobcats are meat eaters. Rodents and rabbits make up the bulk of their diets. They are capable of killing larger prey under ideal conditions — for instance, deer weakened by starvation and hampered by deep snow. Bobcats also have been known to kill and eat porcupines, a dangerous feat that often results in a painful death for the predator.

In an ironic turn of events, the great concern of many Americans for

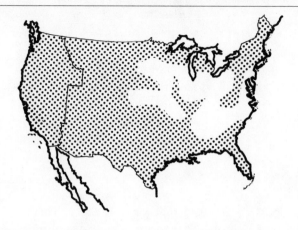

Bobcat range

the plight of the endangered wild cats of the world may be casting a dark cloud on the future of the Bobcat here. The passage of the Endangered Species Act of 1969 effectively stopped the legal importation of the pelts of such dwindling spotted cats as the Leopard, Cheetah, Jaguar, Margay, and Ocelot.

Profit-hungry American furriers, feeling the financial pinch, began promoting Bobcat, once considered almost worthless, as the latest luxury fur. The result has been a manifold increase in the price paid for Bobcat pelts. During the 1951-52 trapping season in California, licensed trappers reported selling only 239 Bobcats that brought an average of 90 cents per pelt. The report for the 1976-77 season showed trappers selling 2,203 Bobcats in California for an average of $133 per pelt.

Unfortunately, the number of Bobcats killed and sold by trappers is only a minor part of the total taken. Hunters in California kill about 10,000 each year and the majority of these also are sold on the fur market.

There is a growing concern for the future of the Bobcat in America. Many conservationists feel that the species should be protected or even put on the threatened species list. The result of this concern is that many state game agencies are belatedly taking a close look at Bobcat population dynamics to determine if legal protection is needed to assure the future of these beautiful and valuable predators.

In myths and legends, the fox is always the cunning villain.

4

A Red Fox is a Rare Sight in California: The state of California has two disjunct (separate) populations of Red Foxes, *Vulpes fulva*, but one may be the result of either accidental or intentional releases from fur farms. The native mountain population ranges from Kern County northward in the Sierra Nevada and Cascades, to Mount Shasta and into Trinity County. A Sacramento Valley population also has been reported, ranging from Yolo to Tehama County.

The Red Fox of California's mountains is found above 5,000 feet and is now a very rare and seldom-observed member of our native fauna (animal life). It lives in the red fir-lodgepole pine and subalpine belts where it hunts a diet of rodents, birds, and insects in montane (mountain zone) chaparral and boulder fields.

The valley Red Fox population is thought to have been introduced in the area from another place. Early writings of explorers and fur trappers made no mention of them. Study skins of valley Red Fox, collected by zoologists at the University of California, Davis, differ from those of the mountain population. The skins of valley foxes appear identical to those of Red Foxes from the Midwest, where stock for fur farms originally was obtained.

The only Red Fox I have ever seen in the valley was at the Sacramento National Wildlife Refuge in Colusa County in 1967.

Of the four species of foxes found in California and on its coastal islands, only the Red Fox has a white tip on its bushy tail. The tiny kit fox of the desert has a distinct black tip; on Island and Gray Foxes, this tip continues as a dark stripe up the center of the tail.

Field identification of the Red Fox is made difficult by the several color phases that can occur. The four phases are the red, cross, silver, and black and these grade insensibly into one another. In the typical red phase, the pelage (coat) is yellowish-red, with black feet, legs, and ear tips. The color tends to be deeper red on the back and more yellowish on the sides — the underparts may be near white.

A cross fox is similar to a red-phase animal except for a dark stripe down the back and one across the shoulders, forming a cross. The black phase is melanistic (black pigmentation), but, like the others, retains the white tail tip. In the silver phase, white-banded guard hairs in an otherwise all-black pelt give a beautiful silvery appearance.

The three atypical (not typical) color phases — cross, silver, and black — were the most valuable in the fur trade, even though the cross fox may have been more common than red phase in the Sierra. Old trappers report that more than half of the Sierran foxes were of the cross phase, about five per cent were silvers, and about one per cent were blacks.

The Red Fox has a natural range greater than any other wild canid, with the possible exception of the original range of the Gray Wolf. It is found throughout almost all of the Northern Hemisphere and it has been introduced to Australia and parts of the Southern Hemisphere by devotees of that curious Anglo-Saxon cult that uses hounds and jumping horses to chase foxes. Like the introduction of European rabbits to Australia, this was a mistake — it has hastened the disappearance of Australia's native marsupial predators.

Like the wolf, the Red Fox has been the subject of myth and legend since the dawn of civilization. It has become the symbol of cunning and resourceful behavior, the villain of all-too-many nursery rhymes and fairy tales. One of the most popular Red Fox stories concerns its supernatural ability to escape hounds. More probably, the fox simply flees for its life as rapidly as possible — its nimble flight crossing barriers that temporarily halt the clumsy dogs. Its cousin, the Gray Fox, never has been a popular victim of horse and hound — it ends the race too quickly by climbing a tree like a cat.

Unlike many of the highly social canids, Red Foxes are usually solitary. There have been reports of more than one vixen raising pups in a single den, but this is probably atypical behavior. Red Foxes seldom are found in larger than family groupings.

Young Red Foxes are born in the spring in a den either dug from

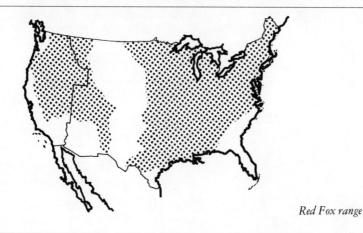

Red Fox range

scratch by the adults or an enlarged rodent or rabbit burrow. In the Sierra, where large boulders are always convenient, they seldom bother to dig a burrow.

A litter of Red Fox pups may number from one to twelve, but five is an average family. Like the pups of domestic dogs, they are born blind and don't open their eyes until about 10 to 15 days of age. By the age of one month, they make their first appearance outside the den and soon will spend many hours each day playing with each other and learning to hunt such formidable prey as grasshoppers and crickets.

Weaning begins at six weeks, when the vixen moves to another nearby den to sleep, but continues to bring solid food to her pups. They slowly learn to hunt for themselves and are usually on their own by four or five months of age. They reach sexual maturity at seven to eleven months.

Naturalists disagree as to the role played by the male Red Fox in helping to raise the young. There is evidence that some males aid in raising pups by bringing food after they are weaned, but this is apparently not true of all males. Some father several litters a year and leave all the domestic chores to the vixens.

Although Red Foxes are predators themselves, they are sometimes eaten by even larger carnivores. The pups are easily taken by Coyotes, Bobcats, and eagles — even the adults sometimes fall victim to eagles.

The extreme rarity of California's Red Foxes has resulted in their removal from the legal-to-kill list. This leaves only the Gray Fox still unprotected in that state. In addition, the California Department of Fish and Game has asked that any sightings of Red Foxes be reported so some idea of the current population and range can be established.

*Feather snowshoes allow them to scamper about on
lightly packed snow.*

5

S ome New Californians: A new
name recently was added to the long list of
birds known to breed in California. This was the White-tailed Ptarmigan,
Lagopus leucurus, a grouse-family member that occupies habitat
uninteresting to most other birds.

In 1971 and 1972, a total of 73 White-tailed Ptarmigans (the p is
silent) were live-trapped in the Rockies of Colorado and released on Eagle
Peak in the Sierra Nevada. This transplant was done by the California
Department of Fish and Game. The stated reason was ". . . to introduce
another game bird in an area lacking a huntable species."

As a follow-up on this experimental relocation, the department hired
two student assistants during the summer of 1976 to survey ptarmigan
habitat near the release point for evidence of breeding success. These young
biologists, Christina Spencer and Vickie Mills, spent two and a half weeks
in some of the West's most spectacular high-country. Their report
indicated that the new colony is healthy and had produced several broods of
chicks during that breeding season.

White-tailed Ptarmigans live only in alpine tundra. This strangely
beautiful plant community is found in the West on the tops of the higher
peaks of the Rockies, Cascades, Northern Coast Ranges, and the Sierra.
Native populations of White-tails are found in New Mexico, Colorado,
Wyoming, Montana, Idaho, Oregon, Washington, Canada, and Alaska,
but this species was strangely missing from California's alpine regions.

Alpine tundra is characterized by long harsh winters, short glorious

31

summers, moderate snowfall, below-zero winter temperatures, and winds of almost unbelievable velocity. No trees are able to grow on this forbidding landscape and the only woody plants are low-growing dwarf willows. These grow only a few centimeters high but provide the ptarmigan with all of its winter food requirements in the form of tender leaf buds.

Despite brutal living conditions, White-tailed Ptarmigans are permanent residents of the alpine tundra and are the only birds known to remain there throughout the year. Their summertime associates, which include Rosy Finches, Horned Larks, Water Pipits, White-crowned Sparrows, and a few others, all fly south or to lower elevations before the first storms of fall leave a mantle of white on the high country.

A cursory examination of the anatomy of a ptarmigan reveals that this bird is not an evolutionary newcomer to its winter-dominated environment. First, as with several arctic animals such as the Ermine, Arctic Fox, and Arctic Hare, it turns pure white in winter. This is a valuable aid in evading the few but hungry predators that remain in the high country at this time. Only the bird's eyes and bill remain dark, and these look like tiny specks of dirt on a snowfield when the bird is motionless.

Another important winter adaptation by ptarmigans is their feathered legs and feet. Their Latin generic name, *Lagopus*, means rabbit footed and refers to these very efficient feather snowshoes which allow the birds to scamper easily about on the surface of lightly packed snow. The foot feathers also perform the essential task of keeping these extremities from freezing when the mercury dips.

Adaptive behavior patterns aid the ptarmigan in winter survival. Rather than shunning the blanket of snow that covers their home area, they plunge beneath it and are completely protected from wind and subzero temperatures. They are able to walk about and even feed below the surface of a light powder snow.

When the snow begins to melt in spring, ptarmigans molt and replace the white feathers on head, back, and upper breast with a plumage of mottled brown. This color combination blends splendidly with the drab browns of the summer tundra and an incubating hen is almost impossible to see on her nest.

Anyone lucky enough to have observed White-tailed Ptarmigans in the high country finds it very difficult to think of them as game birds. I photographed my first ptarmigan in the beautiful Mt. Wilson Primitive Area of the Colorado Rockies several years ago. The bird, a hen in summer

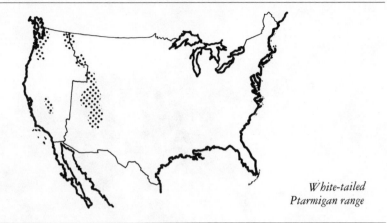

*White-tailed
Ptarmigan range*

plumage, was feeding near a snowbank at about 13,000 feet (4,000 meters) above sea-level on a boulder-strewn slope of Mt. Wilson.

I wasn't carrying a telephoto lens, but was able to photograph her from less that four feet (1.2 meters) with a normal lens. I ran out of film after only two exposures and my extra film was tucked away in a pack on my back. However, my cooperative subject remained motionless almost at my feet as I removed my pack, got out a new roll of film and reloaded. She then held the pose until I had taken all the photographs I wanted.

Game management people claim that ptarmigans will become wilder after they are shot at and will offer hunters a sporting target. They were heavily hunted for food by miners in the Colorado Rockies who called them snow quail, but these pot hunters were probably more interested in their table qualities than in their wariness.

Many attempts at relocating wildlife to provide targets for hunters have resulted in serious impacts upon the pre-existing wildlife communities. It is difficult to determine beforehand just what effects a new species may have on long-established and complex interrelationships.

On the surface, it would appear that few problems are likely to result from a bird with as restricted a habitat requirement as the White-tailed Ptarmigan. However, it is hard to predict the future population dynamics of an animal introduced into a new range. Lack of predators could allow ptarmigan populations to explode in the Sierra and perhaps have an adverse effect on some of the fragile plant life of the alpine tundra.

As exciting as it is to see a new animal in a region where it has not been reported before, I believe most naturalists would agree these introductions are not worth the risk. Game agencies should spend their all-too-limited funds in protecting native wildlife instead of playing Russian roulette with fragile ecosystems.

Moose are the most aquatic of our North American deer.

6

The Largest Antlered Animal:

The Moose, *Alces alces*, has the greatest range of any member of the deer family. It is a circumpolar animal, found throughout the regions of the World in boreal (northern) forests. Some zoologists treat the North American Moose as a distinct species, *Alces americana*, although most consider all Moose as belonging to the same species.

A mix-up in common names of the larger deer species has resulted in some confusion. In Europe, the Moose is called an elk. Their equivalent of our elk is the Red Deer, quite a different species. Many zoologists prefer to call the North American Elk by its Indian name, Wapiti.

The Moose is the largest antlered animal ever to walk on Earth. A large Alaskan bull may weigh 1,500 pounds (680 kilograms) or more and stand eight feet (2.4 meters) high at the withers (shoulders). Its many-pronged, palmated (hand-shaped) antlers may span six feet (1.8 meters) and weigh as much as 85 pounds (38.6 kilograms). The Moose of Canada and the Rocky Mountains are smaller than the Alaskan giants, but the southern bulls still weigh more than 1,000 pounds (454 kilograms).

While the modern Moose is believed to be the heaviest-bodied deer ever to live, its six-foot (2-meter) antlers are dwarfed when compared to those of a relative that lived during the Pleistocene Ice Ages. This great deer, known as the Irish Elk, left fossil remains with fantastic palmated antlers that spanned 11 feet (3.4 meters) from tip to tip, and which probably weighed several hundred pounds.

35

As formidable as those antlers might have looked, they were undoubtedly more a hindrance than an asset when it came to escaping fleet-footed wolves and the spears of early *Homo sapiens*. The Irish Elk often has been pointed out as an example of evolution run wild, but this is probably not really the case at all. More likely this ancient elk developed its great ornamentation during a time when predation pressure was low, and it was a definite advantage in ritualized battles with other bulls. The species became an evolutionary dead end when its strange specialization was no longer an advantage.

With its great gaunt body perched on slender legs, some 4½ feet (1.4 meters) long, it's easy to think what an awkward and ungainly beast a Moose must be. The truth is, a Moose can move about in thick cover as quickly and as quietly as a White-tailed Deer. I am always amazed at how a large bull with a huge spread of antlers can move rapidly through heavy timber without becoming hopelessly entangled.

Moose are the most aquatic of our North American deer and spend a great deal of time feeding in the water. The leaves and buds of willows are a mainstay throughout most of their range and these shrubs grow chiefly along stream banks and on the shallow margins of lakes and ponds.

I had my first close encounter with a Moose while canoeing down Torrey Creek through a beautiful glaciated valley in the Wind River Mountains of Wyoming. The stretch I was paddling meanders through a dense willow thicket that in many places obscures what lies beyond the next bend. The current is swift enough that back-paddling is out of the question and a lone paddler is kept quite busy keeping his craft pointed down the center of the narrow and twisting waterway.

I had been on the lookout for Moose. Cows with calves are often aggressive, and an angry mother can be a formidable adversary if one can't find a handy tree to climb. At this particular moment, however, I was engrossed in watching for mink along the undercut stream bank. I rounded a bend and looked up to see what appeared to be four small tree trunks growing out of the center of the stream. Perched atop these slender stems was a cow Moose that, from my low vantage point, appeared to be 10 feet (3 meters) tall even though she was standing in three feet (1 meter) of water.

I was scant yards away when I saw the Moose and had only seconds to figure out how to pass her in the narrow channel. She apparently had just stepped off the bank to my right and was wading toward the left-hand bank. Hoping she wouldn't change her mind and turn back, I made one desperate drawstroke that sent the canoe through an eight-foot gap between her hind end and the right bank. I easily could have swatted her

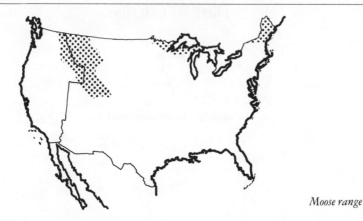

Moose range

on the rump with the canoe paddle as I passed. But I let discretion overrule valor and beat a hasty retreat downstream.

I have had other encounters with Moose since, and even have been chased by an antlered bull, but none of these was as thrilling as sneaking past that surprised cow in Torrey Creek. She showed no sign of aggression as I passed. When I finally looked back, all I saw was a dark form disappearing into the willows on the opposite side of the creek. If she had a calf, I didn't see it.

Bull Moose do not assemble a harem as do elk, but they do become quite bellicose (quarrelsome) during the fall rutting season which may last two months. They tend to treat any large moving object as a sexual rival and have even attacked railroad locomotives moving slowly down the track.

Outside of armed men, against whom they have no chance, the only serious predator a Moose must face are wolves. Wolves and Moose have evolved together over thousands of years and have established a predatory-prey relationship that is beneficial to both. Without the Moose to provide large quantities of protein, pack-hunting wolves could not survive in the boreal forests. Without wolves, sick and old Moose would live longer and consume food needed by younger and healthier animals.

In North America, the Moose is found throughout the boreal forests of Alaska and Canada and down into the northern tier of states. In the West, it is found in the Rocky Mountain regions of Montana, Idaho, Wyoming, and eastern Washington.

In the area near Yellowstone National Park in Wyoming, Moose are a common sight in roadside meadows. "Moose jams" often result when tourists begin stopping in the middle of the highway and jumping out of their cars and recreational vehicles to gawk at or photograph them.

7

Termites - Master Architects and Wreckers: It is a strange twist of fate that

the insect group most often to blame for destroying the architectural efforts of humans includes some of the most skillful builders found in the nonhuman world. I'm writing, of course, of termites, a very primitive insect order that has the rather rare ability to digest cellulose, the organic compound of which all wood and wood products is composed.

Although termites often are called white ants, these two distinct groups of social insects are not closely related. Ants are Hymenopterans, members of a highly advanced order that includes the bees and wasps. Termites are Isopterans, a very primitive group that evolved from cockroach-like ancestors several hundreds of millions years ago.

Predating both ants and bees, termites are considered the first living organisms to evolve a social lifestyle — a system in which the work load is shared by each member of a colony, and complex behavior patterns are designed to benefit the group rather than the individual.

Some 2,000 species of termites have been classified, the majority of them tropical. A few have invaded temperate climes, and the United States and Canada share about 50 of these. Although they have a terrible reputation as home wreckers, only two of the genera (groups) found in this country have members that attack human abodes. These are the Subterranean or Damp Wood Termites in genus *Reticulitermes*, and the Dry Wood Termites in *Kalotermes*. The Damp Woods nest in moist soil but tunnel up into wood to feed, while the Dry Woods live and feed in dry

Most termites spend their lives in the forest.

wood without need for a connection with the soil.

The majority of termites spend their lives as important decomposing organisms of forest ecosystems, never invading humans' buildings. They are necessary first links in a complex chain of living creatures whose task is the vital one of converting nutrients locked in dead wood into basic elemental materials that can be recycled. Without the decomposers, all living systems would grind to a halt when essential raw materials became unavailable.

The termite's ability to extract energy from normally indigestible cellulose is the result of a relationship, called symbiosis, between these social insects and tiny single-celled protozoans living in their intestinal tracts. These protozoans produce an enzyme which can convert the cellulose eaten by the termites into sugar. This easily digested carbohydrate is then used as food, both by the termites and their tiny symbionts.

The protozoans found in termites are not capable of independent existence. Young termites are not hatched with these important organisms in their gut, but obtain them by eating fecal (bodily waste) matter from adult members of the colony.

One way termites differ from ants is in their incomplete metamorphosis. Ants have the typical egg-larva-pupa-adult life cycle we have grown accustomed to associating with insect life histories. Termites skip the pupal stage. Their eggs hatch into nymphs, much like adults except for their smaller size.

As part of a highly developed social order, termites have a caste system. Each colony consists of several different-appearing types, each with its own function. Manual labor is performed by a worker caste that has well-developed jaws for chewing wood and working on construction projects. Some termite species use child labor only — their workers are all juveniles that will grow up to become members of the reproductive caste. In other species, the workers are permanently sterile and wingless individuals that labor until death sets them free.

Some termite nymphs develop into soldiers, both male and female but always sterile. Soldiers have elongated heads with either a powerful pair of biting jaws or a snout that tapers to form a spray nozzle. The job of the soldiers is to attack and repel any invaders entering the colony. Those with nozzle heads, known as nasutes, spray a sticky substance that quickly immobilizes most small insect predators.

The breeding chores of a termite colony are assigned to members of the reproductive caste. These develop wings when they mature and go on mass nuptial flights during which they pair off and seek sites for new colonies. Unlike bees, which mate only on the nuptial flight (the queen bee carries sperm from her first and only mating in her body for the rest of her life), termite pairs form a lifelong bond, but don't mate until they are located in their new home.

These founding pairs, which lose their wings soon after the nuptial flight, are placed in a royal cell by their first offspring. Here the female becomes a sausage-like blob, nothing much but an egg-laying machine. In some of the larger species she may be four inches in length and may lay more than one-million eggs during a 15- to 50-year lifespan.

For years one of the most baffling aspects of termite natural history was the manner in which genetically identical eggs produced by the queen develop into the correct proportion of soldiers, workers, and reproductives for a smooth functioning colony. Experimenters have determined that this selective development is accomplished by chemicals called pheromones. These special hormones released by members of each caste act to inhibit the development of more members of that caste. Thus, when the number of soldiers in a colony is low, the quantity of soldier-inhibiting pheromone also will be low. More eggs will develop into soldiers until an increase in the pheromone again slows down their production.

Secondary reproductives, which do not grow wings, are kept on hand to replace the king or queen if they should die.

Although our native termites build elaborate systems of galleries in dead wood or below ground, we must look to tropical varieties to really appreciate the architectural instincts evolved by these remarkable insects. Many of these build mound-like termite cities called termitaria that reach amazing size. One African species builds mounds 20 feet (6.1 meters) in height and 12 feet (4 meters) in diameter. They have concrete-like walls two feet (61 centimeters) thick and are all but impervious to anything but dynamite or the claws of the Aardvark.

More astounding than sheer size of the termitaria are their beautifully designed heating and ventilating systems. Heat energy is provided by the metabolic activity of the million or more members of the colony and of the fungi they cultivate in carefully tended mushroom cellars. The heated air rises to the attic of the termite mound where it is forced under convective pressure down through a skillfully constructed ductwork system that cools, humidifies, and extracts the excess carbon dioxide before it is recycled.

Every bit of waste material, including fecal matter, in these African colonies is used as building material or as compost to grow mushrooms upon which the termites partially subsist. Deep wells, that may extend more than 100 feet (30 meters) down, provide the water necessary for the colony. Trails lead from the mound to nearby sources of food material that is carried back by workers to provide the basic source of energy for the colony.

Always give Black Bear cubs a wide berth in the woods.

8

B lack Bears Aren't Always Black:
Black Bears, *Ursus americana*, can be found
almost anywhere in the West where a significant amount of coniferous
forest remains. They are most numerous in the Sierra Nevada, the northern
Coastal Ranges, and in the Cascades, but still can be found in the San
Gabriel and San Bernardino Mountains in populous Southern California.

The Black Bear inherited the title of California's largest carnivorous
land animal when the magnificent California Grizzly was exterminated by
hunters in the 1920s. A large male Black Bear may tip the scales at more
than 500 pounds (227 kilograms), still a dwarf when compared to the
1,000-pound (454-kilogram) "golden bear" that posthumously became
California's official state mammal.

Almost everyone has seen Black Bears in zoos or in our national parks.
However, one misconception regarding their color should be mentioned.
The cinnamon or dark-brown animals many think are a different species of
bear are really just color phases of old *Ursus americana*. These light phases
are more common than the black phase in the West. Cubs from a single
litter may be of more than one color phase. A beautiful blue race, called the
glacier bear, is found in southeastern Alaska.

Wilderness Black Bears are shy and retiring animals that normally flee
at the first sight, sound, or smell of humans. Park Black Bears are a
different story — they have learned that campers and backpackers are an
easy source of food and many vacations have been cut short when an old
bruin ate up all the grub.

Locking up food in an automobile is not always a deterrent to these resourceful freeloaders. Yosemite bears have learned to remove the glass from automobile windows. An ice chest left out at night offers no challenge at all.

Hanging food in a tree is not very effective — Black Bears are excellent climbers, both as cubs and as adults. (Adult Grizzlies can't climb unless a tree has many limbs close to the ground.) Backpackers usually carry a stout length of rope to suspend their packs between two trees at night. Even this technique no longer works in all cases, as some bears have learned to climb up and chew off one end of the rope.

Phyllis and I observed a Yosemite Black Bear in action while backpacking in the backcountry of this popular park. We had hung our food in a nylon bag suspended by a rope from a large dead lodgepole pine. The pine had fallen against another tree at about a 45-degree angle.

Sometime during the night we were awakened by the sound of claws raking dead wood. A flashlight beam revealed the source. A large bear lay across the sloping log swinging the rope from which the food hung about six feet (1.8 meters) below its reach. When it became obvious the midnight raider would be successful — we didn't want to subsist on pine nuts and wild onions on our hike out — we shouted and banged a spoon on an aluminum plate. Looking like a big kid caught with his hand in the cookie jar, the bear backed down the tree and ambled off into the night. Most bears don't give up that easily and we were surprised he didn't come back and try again.

Feeding bears in our national parks is not just illegal, it is highly dangerous. They may seem completely docile as long as the food holds out, but many tourists have been injured when the goody supply failed to match the bear's appetite. In an effort to force them to find wild food, the National Park Service has phased out the open garbage pits that once attracted many bears. This phase-out was accomplished too quickly, and has resulted in an increased incidence of bear-human encounters as more bears have turned to campground raiding as a substitute for the garbage dumps.

Another misconception about bears is that they hibernate. True hibernation is found in mammals such as the Golden-mantled Squirrel which experiences a lowering of body temperature and goes into a state of almost complete suspended animation during its winter sleep — only the pilot light of its internal furnace is left burning. Bears do sleep for varying periods of time during cold weather, but their body temperature remains normal and they can quickly awaken if disturbed in their dens.

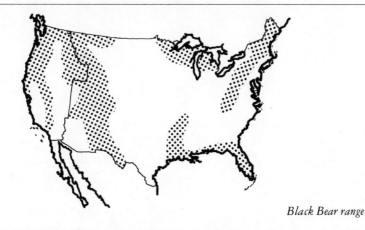

Black Bear range

Pregnant females go into their winter sleep earlier than other bears, and their cubs are born sometime in January — usually twins, but triplets are not uncommon. Blind, toothless, hairless, only nine inches (23 centimeters) long and six ounces (170 grams) in weight, a Black Bear cub at birth is hardly a suggestion of the powerful 300- to 500-pound (136 to 227 kilogram) animal it may become. Through the long and cold winter, the cubs survive and gain weight by nursing, using the energy stored in their mother's thick layer of fat.

When spring at last arrives, a much slimmer mother bear leads her new family — each cub is now about four pounds in weight — out of the den for a first look at the great outdoors. At this time a Black Bear sow can be the most dangerous. She is very protective and may attack without warning if her cubs are approached too closely. Wise outdoor people always give bear cubs encountered in the woods a wide berth. Mama is never far off.

Black Bears are fascinating members of our wildlife community and offer a great deal of enjoyment to watchers. They present little danger to woodland visitors who keep a few basic rules in mind: Don't feed them. Stay away from cubs. Don't use a slab of bacon as a pillow under your sleeping bag.

A Wolverine looks something like a small bear.

9

Arch-Villain of Old Trappers' Tales: The Wolverine, *Gulo luscus*, is cast as the heavy in a lot of old trapper stories of the Far North. Just how many of the almost supernatural feats attributed to this large member of the weasel family have any basis in fact always creates lively debate among naturalists.

The Wolverine looks something like a small bear. It is squat and powerful — an adult male may weigh 25 to 35 pounds (11.3 to 16 kilograms) and be more than three feet (91.4 centimeters) long, but will stand 15 inches (38 centimeters) at the shoulders. Its feet are large for an animal its size, and its tracks easily might be mistaken for a Timber Wolf if the fifth toe (all canine tracks show only four toes) of the Wolverine fails to leave an impression.

Wolverine fur is long and silky and dark brown in color. A tan stripe on either side of the body extends on to the top surface of the tail. The head is grizzled gray with a black muzzle.

There is no doubt the Wolverine is a powerful animal for its size. Great strength is a characteristic of the weasel family; the Wolverine's smaller cousin, the Badger, is another notable example of this. However, the tales of a Wolverine chasing a Grizzly Bear away from its kill or whipping two wolves at once leave some room for doubt.

Adolp Murie, who spent many years in Alaska as a field biologist for the National Park Service, felt that the Wolverine was overrated as a fighter. He wrote of several instances where tracks in the snow had shown that a single wolf had pursued a Wolverine, and the Wolverine had needed all its power to escape.

Another popular Wolverine story has to do with their ability to run a trapper out of business by stealing his baits, eating his victims, and hiding his traps without ever getting caught themselves (how I wish this one were true.) The fact that many pelts of trapped Wolverine are traded on the fur market is evidence they are not invincible.

Wolverine fur usually is used for the ruff on arctic parkas because it reportedly will not ice up like other furs. Murie, who wore a Wolverine-edged parka hood for his winter field work in Alaska, reported that his did, in fact, ice up.

A popular common name for the Wolverine is glutton, to commemorate its almost mythical ability to put away huge quantities of food at one time. Old trappers tell of Wolverines that ate a whole Moose in one meal, or of having their entire winter's food supply consumed or ruined by one Wolverine during a cabin break-in.

There is probably some basis for these tales, because, like all members of the weasel family, Wolverines have a very high metabolism. They must search for food almost continually during waking hours to keep their internal furnaces stoked — especially during the frigid arctic winters. However, Murie's observations disagreed with these fanciful tales. He felt that a Wolverine consumed little more food than would be expected for an animal its size, but like a dog, it would gorge when given the opportunity.

Most range maps for the Wolverine in North America show it occurring throughout most of Canada, Alaska, and extending down into the lower 48 in the Cascade, Sierra Nevada, and Rocky Mountains. There has been controversy recently regarding Wolverines in California. They probably never were very numerous and are extremely rare today.

The Wolverine is on the list of rare animals compiled by the California Department of Fish and Game, and is a fully protected animal. This agency reports there have been 87 sightings of Wolverine since 1950 — 27 of these since 1970.

My own conversations with persons who have reported Wolverines in the Sierra make me a little doubtful about their accuracy. In almost every case, I felt that what really was seen was a Yellow-bellied Marmot.

Distances are deceiving in the high country, and a marmot at close range can look like a larger animal farther away. This was brought home to me in 1971, when I investigated a report of a Mountain Lion sighting by a couple attending Audubon Camp of the West in the Wind River Mountains where I was a staff member. The only tracks I could find in the

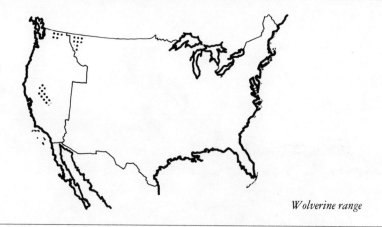

Wolverine range

trail where they said the lion had crossed were those of a marmot. However, I couldn't convince them they hadn't seen a lion — and maybe they had.

I have hiked the Sierra for more than 30 years and one of my greatest desires has been to see a Wolverine or its tracks. I have never found a single track of these mysterious animals, but I haven't given up hope.

The pad prints of a Wolverine, if in mud or snow, will show five toe prints, with a distinct claw mark in front of each. The front paw shows a heel print and will leave a track five to six inches (13 to 15 centimeters) long and four to five inches (10 to 13 centimeters) wide. The hind paw track will be three to four inches (8 to 10 centimeters) long by four to five inches (10 to 13 centimeters) wide.

The flying squirrel steers with its tail.

10

A Furry Magic Carpet: The lovely little elf-like flying squirrels are Nature's living magic carpets. They lack the ability of true powered flight, which has been perfected only by birds, bats, and insects, but are able to glide for astounding distances after launching themselves from a suitable height.

Throughout the world, some 37 species of flying squirrels have been classified, but only two are found in North America. Ours is the Northern Flying Squirrel, *Glaucomys sabrinus*, which occurs in the Sierra Nevada and Rocky Mountains, north to Alaska, and throughout the boreal (northern) forests of Canada and the United States.

Our flying squirrel is tiny compared to many of its relatives. An adult will measure four or five inches (10 to 13 centimeters) in body length, with its flattened tail adding a like amount. In contrast, the giant flying squirrel of southeastern Asia is four feet (1.2 meters) in overall length.

Flying squirrels glide on a thin web of skin stretched between outspread legs. This provides a relatively large, rectangular airfoil, over which is spread their few ounces of body weight. Unlike the naked wings of bats, the gliding surfaces of flying squirrels are covered with the same soft and luxurious olive-gray fur as the rest of their bodies.

The ability of flying squirrels goes beyond simply gliding from a high perch to land on the ground below. They are capable of very precise maneuvers accomplished by raising and lowering their "wings" and using the tail as a rudder. They can dive steeply to increase momentum in order to soar steeply upward before landing. They usually pick a tree trunk as a landing field and swing their bodies into a vertical position to land on all four feet.

Just as with human piloted hang-gliders, aerobatics are not beyond the grasp of flying squirrels. They have been observed making tight turns, lateral loops, and spiraling dives. If they change their minds after take off, they can turn back and land on the same limb.

Their large liquid eyes, which give flying squirrels such an endearing look, are indicative of their nocturnal life style. They are seldom seen during daylight hours unless disturbed from their nests in tree cavities or of leafy stick construction, much like those built by other tree squirrels. They start their nighttime foraging after the sun goes down and return to daytime hiding places before the first crack of dawn.

Their nocturnal habits make flying squirrels appear far less common than they actually are. Biologists have discovered they average three individuals per acre of suitable habitat. They are highly gregarious — many may share a single old snag that is riddled with woodpecker nests or natural cavities.

Nuts and seeds make up the bulk of flying squirrels' diets, but they seldom pass up the opportunity for higher protein meals when available. They eat many insects and spider-egg cases and are known to feed on the eggs and young of birds. They often are caught in meat-baited traps set for other animals. Crackers, nuts, or other goodies left around a camp at night often are gone the next morning with flying squirrels the likely culprits.

The instinct to hoard food is deeply ingrained in flying squirrels, and reaches almost a frenzy in fall when nuts and seeds are ripe. One investigator found that a squirrel that gathered and hid 20 nuts per night in summer increased this effort to 270 per night in November. Nuts and seeds usually are buried under leaf litter or hidden in cracks or hollows in tree trunks. Many, forgotten by these little hoarders, sprout to become new forest trees.

Northern Flying Squirrels mate in late winter. The young are born in spring after a gestation period of about 40 days. They are altricial — born naked, blind, and helpless. They first open their eyes at three and a half to four weeks of age, and by six to eight weeks look much like their parents and are taking their first short "flights."

Their speed and agility, combined with nocturnal habits, make Northern Flying Squirrels relatively safe from most predators. The major threat is the larger owls, which hunt at times when flying squirrels are most active. Many squirrel skulls are found in the regurgitation pellets of Great Horned and Spotted Owls.

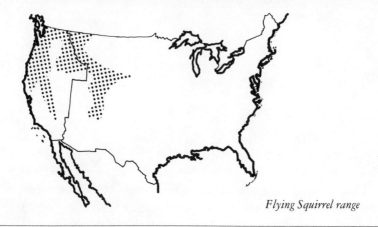

Flying Squirrel range

Flying squirrels prefer coniferous forests with some scattered hardwoods that are more apt to have cavities for nests. When they take up residence in the attics of mountain cabins they can be heard coming and going during the night.

In the Sierra and the Rockies, flying squirrels are found from the lower edge of the ponderosa pine belt to the upper edge of the red fir-lodgepole pine belt.

Weasels follow rodent prey right into their burrows.

11

C uriosity is a Weasel Trait: As a youngster growing up in the urban wilds of Los Angeles, I had little opportunity to observe predatory mammals, except for domestic cats and dogs. One of my greatest thrills was the discovery of a weasel living in a large vacant field behind our home.

I found my weasel one morning when, instead of trotting off in the direction of the neighborhood school as I was supposed to, I was hopelessly sidetracked by a pile of fresh dirt at an open gopher hole. Lying in the dewy grass, I patiently awaited a glimpse of the gopher when it brought up another load of soil.

What finally appeared at the open hole was not a chunky pocket gopher, but the tiny head and slender neck of an animal I had never seen before. In disbelief, I stared into a pair of alert black eyes from a distance of less than four feet. My weasel appeared curious but not fearful.

Suddenly, with a motion too fast for my wondering eyes to follow, the tiny form disappeared, leaving me staring down an empty hole and thinking I had imagined the whole thing.

After I contemplated it for a while, I felt certain my mystery animal was a weasel, but it required a trip to the library to find out which species. This, my first weasel, was easy to identify, for it was of the bridled color phase of the Longtail Weasel, *Mustela frenata*, the common form in the Southwest. A large white spot in the middle of the forehead and a white stripe in front of each ear give this beautifully marked variety a very distinctive appearance.

Weasels belong to a diverse family of carnivores called the Mustelidae. The family name derives from the presence of well-developed musk glands. In skunks, these glands have been perfected as highly efficient defense weapons. Weasels lack the musk guns of skunks but can exude an odor I think is even more unpleasant than that of their black-and-white cousins.

Only two of North America's three species of weasels are widely distributed in the West. The Longtail, which I discovered in that weedy vacant lot in Los Angeles, is the most common. The Ermine or Shorttail Weasel, *Mustela erminea*, coexists with its Longtail cousin in the Rockies and the Pacific Northwest. The Least Weasel, *Mustela rixosa*, is common in the Great Lakes region, but just penetrates the West in northern Montana.

Northern California represents the southern tip of a vast area covered by the Ermine. The area includes the northern states, almost all of Canada, Alaska, and the north coastal region of Greenland. The Longtail is found over an equally large, but more temperate region, from southern Canada to Central America.

Weasels are slender, short-legged hunters that are beautifully adapted for their major function as predator of small rodents. They are able to follow prey right into their burrows, while larger carnivores, such as Coyotes or Badgers, must catch them outside or dig them out.

An adult Longtail Weasel is eight to ten inches (20 to 25 centimeters) long, with a three- to six-inch (7 to 15 centimeters) black-tipped tail. The Shorttail is slightly smaller. Where their ranges overlap, as in the northern Sierra, the Longtail does not occur in the bridled color phase, making it more difficult to tell them apart.

During the summer, both Shorttail and Longtail Weasels are brown above and very light-colored below. The belly, throat, and feet of the Shorttail are snowy white, while the underparts of the Longtail may be white or yellow with brown feet.

During the winter in the snowy parts of their ranges, both Longtails and Shorttails turn pure white except for the black tip on their tails. The Least Weasel also turns white, but lacks the black tail tip. The white winter pelts of all weasels are sold as ermine in the fur trade.

Weasels have a bad reputation, which they don't really deserve, of being wanton killers. An occasional individual may take a liking to domestic poultry and wreak havoc in a hen house, but this behavior is not typical of the whole clan. Mice, rats, and other small rodents are their major source of food. They are capable of killing larger prey — animals as large as Snowshoe Hare may be taken when food is scarce.

Weasels will get greedy when there is an abundance of prey, and kill

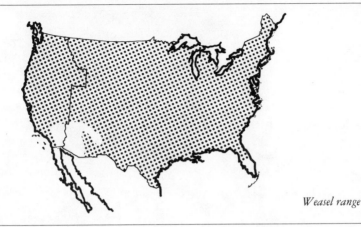

Weasel range

more than they can eat at the time. They sometimes store this extra food in their dens to be eaten later, and it is not uncommon to see weasels carrying rodents in their powerful little jaws as they head home after a successful hunt.

Curiosity is a trait of the weasel clan and makes them easy to observe at close range. Several years ago, while on a field trip in the Colorado Rockies, my students and I enjoyed a game of hide-and-seek with a Shorttail Weasel in a pile of weathered boards at an old ghost town. Each time I made a mouse-like squeak, the little hunter would stick its head out in a different location and fearlessly look us over. Everyone with a camera got good weasel photographs, but my camera was back in the bus a half-mile away.

Although weasels hunt day and night, they are not seen very often. They never are numerous, probably due to their predatory life-style. It takes a lot of mice to feed a voracious weasel that daily consumes half its weight in food, so each animal requires a sizable hunting ground.

Weasels don't hibernate — they can be found seeking food in all kinds of weather. I have followed their tiny tracks on showshoes on many occasions, and always have been fascinated by the random nature of their wanderings. They seem to follow no particular route and often cross and recross their own tracks. They seldom fail to investigate any bit of cover that might hide warm-blooded prey.

Although fierce hunters themselves, weasels are often eaten by larger predators. They are no match for big soaring hawks, such as the Red-tail, and their tiny skulls are sometimes found in the regurgitation pellets of these birds. When hunting at night, weasels are an easy victim of the silent and deadly swoop of the Great Horned Owl.

The Saw-whet Owl has a bat-like appearance as it
flits through the deepening shadows of dusk.

12

T ecolotito Cabezon, The Little
Big-Headed Owl: The tame and trusting
nature of the tiny Saw-whet Owl, *Aegolius acadicus*, no doubt has
contributed to the myth that owls see poorly or are blind in daylight. If
one is lucky enough to find one of these appealing little gnomes roosting in
the branches of a low tree, it often can be picked up, examined closely, and
put back without its doing more than snapping its bill and blinking its big
yellow eyes to show it was disturbed by the experience.

This lack of fear of humans is not limited to daylight hours when
Saw-whets are sleeping off the fatigue of a hard night of mousing. They
have been known to join campers sitting around a late evening fire and
perch on someone's shoulder while enjoying the dancing flames.

Like the Mountain Lion, the Saw-whet Owl is known by many
different local names over its broad range in North America. To the
French-Canadians it is *la petite nyctale*, "the little night owl". The
Mexican-Indians know it as *tecolotito cabezon,* or "little big-headed owl".

Many early bird books call it the Acadian Owl, in keeping with its
trivial scientific name, *acadicus*, which means "of Acadia." The first
specimen was collected in that region of Nova Scotia immortalized in
Longfellow's poem, *Evangeline*. Acadia comes from a Micmac Indian word
acadie, meaning "fertile land".

The current common name, Saw-whet Owl, results from one version of
this species' large repertoire of calls. This call, heard mostly during the
courtship period in March and April, is a monotonous series of two notes.

"SWEEE-awww SWEEE-awww," that sounds remarkably like the up-and-down stroke of a file on a coarse-toothed cross-cut saw, a sound that is rapidly fading from our memories due to an abomination called the chain saw. This and other calls of the Saw-whet have a remarkable ventriloquial quality that makes the source very difficult to locate.

Saw-whets are tiny owls, about the size of a fat sparrow, and weigh between three and four ounces (85 to 113 grams). Their head is large and rounded and lacks ear tufts. The square tail is very short compared to body size and this contributes to the big-headed appearance. The broad 18-inch (46-centimeter) wings seem much too large for the little body and, combined with the short tail, give them a bat-like appearance as they flit through the deepening shadows of dusk or first gray light of dawn.

The small size, cryptic coloring, nocturnal lifestyle, and fondness for roosting in dense cover make Saw-whet Owls very difficult to find. In coniferous forests, where they are more numerous than many people realize, the best way to see one is to arise before dawn and look at the very tips of tall fir trees. They are fond of greeting the new day from a lofty perch before retiring and can often be seen silhouetted against the light eastern sky.

Another way to find a Saw-whet is to wander around tapping on trees which have old woodpecker holes in their trunks. You may get some strange looks from other hikers, but just ignore their stares and comments about your sanity. Saw-whets and other small owls often nest or roost in these cavities and will sometimes look out to see who is rapping at the front door. My only photographs of a Saw-whet were obtained in this way — I put my camera on a tripod, focused on the opening and took a picture each time it stuck its head out to answer my knock.

One of the most endearing characteristics of Saw-whets is their habit of holding their heads in all sorts of strange positions as they size up an intruder in their domain. They sometimes will bend over so far that their chin appears to rest on their toes, or they may turn their head completely upside-down so their hooked bill appears above their big yellow eyes. The eyes of owls do not rotate in their sockets, so owls must turn their heads to follow whatever they are looking at.

Juvenile Saw-whets look different than adults and at one time were thought to be an entirely different species. Adults are heavily streaked with brown and white on their undersides, but juveniles are an almost uniform mahogany brown except for a striking white triangle above the bill and between the eyes. The youngsters undergo a complete molt in July or August of their first year before they get their first winter plumage and

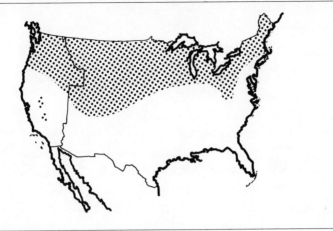

*Saw-whet
Owl range*

from then on they are dead-ringers for their parents.

Saw-whets feed mostly on mice but will take other, sometimes much larger, prey when the small rodents are scarce. There are reports of them killing cottontail rabbits and domestic pigeons, as well as such fierce hunters as the Short-tail Weasel. These little owls have an appetite inversely proportional to their size and may consume up to twice their own weight in one night.

The main enemies of Saw-whets are the larger owls, such as the Great Horned and Spotted, both of which share their forest habitat. Many also die during harsh winters when deep snow makes it difficult for them to find enough food.

Saw-whet Owls are resident species across the northern United States and southern Canada. They are mainly winter visitors to the lowland areas of the West with breeding populations in the mountains. They are not well organized migrants, but seem to just drift southward during times of food scarcity. Birds are usually little affected by adverse weather if they can find sufficient food. If food is scarce, they quickly succumb to the cold.

A biological clock tells the Golden-mantled Squirrel when to hibernate.

13

No Need to Tell Them It's
Spring: The lives of all organisms, from
microbes to humans, are governed by a complex system of rhythmically
repeated events. Birds awaken and sing when dawn interrupts the darkness
of night. Night creatures hasten to daytime dens, to fall fast asleep before
the first glow appears on the eastern horizon.

The lengthening days of early spring see migrant birds winging
northward and hibernating mammals stirring deep in their burrows. Sap
begins to flow upward through the stems of deciduous trees and new leaves
appear almost overnight. Juvenile insects that spent the winter as dormant
pupae, suddenly split their prisons and emerge as beautifully winged
adults.

Governing these cyclical events are the movements of planet Earth
relative to our master energy source, the sun, and to a lesser extent, the
moon. They set the days, the nights, the tides, the seasons.

A fascinating aspect of the periodic behavior patterns of living things is
the apparent independence from external stimuli. It has been demonstrated
many times that organisms isolated from all known external pacesetters
continue to exhibit their cyclical activity patterns.

For instance, a flying squirrel, if kept under conditions of constant
darkness, becomes active after sunset even though it has no visual contact
with the outside world. Tidepool organisms removed from the sea and
placed in aquaria continue cyclical behavior in rhythm with tides — now
unseen and unfelt — that control their lives under natural conditions.

There are so many examples of rhythms persisting long after laboratory isolation that biologists have postulated the existence of internal biological clocks. The most evident of these keeps pace with the 24-hour daily cycle and maintains what has become known as circadian (about a day) rhythm.

The exact mechanism of the biological clock is unknown, but many researchers feel it exists on a molecular level and may function by a principle of oscillation, such as with a pendulum.

Just as mechanical clocks vary in accuracy, biological clocks of living organisms get out of synchronization after long periods of isolation and sometimes appear to run down completely. Under natural conditions, biological clocks are reset by the rhythmical stimuli they keep time with, just as we reset our watches with a master clock on occasion.

The existence of the daily biological clock has been known for a long time. More recently, it was discovered that some animals have an annual clock as well. This discovery was first made at Toronto University where zoologists were studying hibernation habits of a common Western mammal, the Golden-mantled Squirrel, *Citellus laterallis*.

Their tiny captive was kept prisoner in a windowless room maintained at exactly 32 degrees Fahrenheit (zero degrees Celsius) and with 12 hours of artificial light each day. Throughout the summer, although subjected to freezing cold, the squirrel went about its usual activities and maintained a normal body temperature of 98.6 degrees Fahrenheit (37 degrees Celsius).

Then, to the amazement of researchers, when autumn arrived the Golden-mantled Squirrel stopped eating, its body temperature plummeted to two degrees above freezing, and it showed all of the characteristics of a hibernating animal. With its artificial quarters still maintained at 32 degrees and with 12 hours of darkness followed by 12 of light, the tiny subject slept peacefully for the long Canadian winter with which it had no contact.

The following April, still in complete isolation from the lengthening days of spring, the squirrel awoke. Within two hours its body temperature was elevated to normal and it was eating and actively running about its icy quarters.

Not content with the first results, the experimenters kept the squirrel for another season. Again, precisely as if in a natural environment, it went into hibernation in October and awoke in April.

In order to determine whether this amazing annual clock was acquired by heredity or by contact with seasonal environment, the experiment was repeated with baby squirrels born in this artificial environment. They had never seen the light of a normal day or experienced normal seasons. These

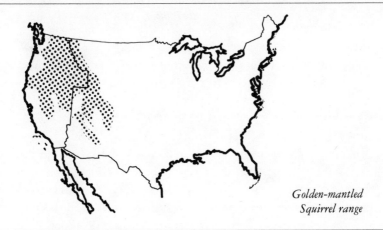

*Golden-mantled
Squirrel range*

also went into hibernation right on schedule and woke up again in perfect synchrony with their free-living relatives in the outside world.

The advantages of an annual biological clock are many. Animals may begin to prepare for coming seasonal events before they actually occur, such as putting on fat in late summer in preparation for winter hibernation. Birds and migratory mammals are able to start their annual treks ahead of winter's first storms which otherwise might catch them with their food supply under several feet of ice and snow.

When a hornet queen awakens from her winter sleep
she is alone.

14

A ncient Papermaker: The art of papermaking was discovered long before our anthropoid ancestors freed their hands for tool-using by learning to walk upright. The first papermakers were not intelligent primates taking advantage of newly acquired brain power and dexterous thumbed hands, but primitive insects functioning entirely by stereotyped behavior patterns that operate beyond the control of conscious thought.

Of the several groups of insects that have "learned" to build shelters out of paper, the best known are hornets. However, they are even better known for another ability — delivering a painful sting to the exposed anatomy of anyone who foolishly wanders too near their closely guarded paper houses.

Papermaking hornets belong to a group of stinging insects known as the social wasps. Closely related to the highly social bees and ants, these wasps have evolved a complex and matriarchal type of society in which efforts of individuals are directed toward the betterment of the community rather than personal gain.

The terms hornet and yellow jacket usually are used interchangeably, but they do denote two closely related but slightly different types of papermaking wasps. Yellow jackets normally build nests below ground in old rodent burrows while hornets suspend theirs from a branch of a tree or other above-ground structure.

The colors yellow and black are usually associated with hornets and yellow jackets although a common species in the West — the Bald-faced

Hornet — is usually black and white. All fold their wings fan-like in the longitudinal direction when at rest. Most are large, ranging from ½ to ¾ of an inch (13 to 19 millimeters) in body length.

Unlike a hive of domestic honey bees whose single queen may live and reproduce for many years, a hornet colony is strictly an annual affair. The old queen dies in late fall and new queens survive the winter to single-handedly found new queendoms the following spring.

When a hornet queen awakens from her long winter sleep she is very much alone. Even the drone who contributed his sperm to the gene pool of the yet-to-be-established colony died soon after the queen's first and only mating the previous fall.

The new queen seeks a suitable location for her paper nest. She quickly collects woodpulp and masticates it with her powerful jaws to a thick papier-mâché.

The new nest begins as a thin stem hanging downward from a tree limb or sometimes from a shed or porch roof. To the free end of the stem she attaches several vertically oriented brood cells, formed in the well-known honeycomb shape. She then molds an egg-shaped outer envelope, with bottom entrance, to weatherproof the brood cells.

Her initial construction completed, she gets down to the business of raising some help. In each brood cell she lays a single egg that quickly will hatch into a maggot-like larva and be completely dependent on her hunting ability until it pupates and becomes a winged adult. She captures insects and chews them into bite-sized pellets to feed to her offspring.

When her first brood — all worker-caste females — reaches adulthood, they take over the task of enlarging the nest as well as providing food for later broods. The queen soon loses her ability to fly and becomes simply an egg-laying machine producing up to 25,000 offspring before the cold days of fall terminate her life.

A second and larger tier of brood chambers is constructed beneath the first, and each receives a fertilized egg that will produce a worker female. As the nest increases in size, new outer walls are added, but portions of the old are retained for insulation.

As new broods of workers emerge from their cocoons, they take turns at guarding the nest, hunting for food, feeding the larvae, building brood chambers, and remodeling the walls. These tasks go faster with more help and by late summer the colony may number several thousand individuals and the paper nest may reach the size of a basketball.

Suddenly, cued by some as yet unknown signal, the workers begin building larger brood cells than those in which they were hatched. In some of these the queen will lay fertilized eggs, and in others the eggs will be unfertilized. The fertilized eggs, identical to those that produced workers earlier in the summer, will develop into queens. The unfertilized eggs will become drones — males whose sole purpose in life is to mate with the new queens to perpetuate the species.

The hornets practice a form of energy conservation by waiting until late summer to produce drones and queens. Neither of these castes was needed earlier in the season and would have just consumed food needed for the active workers.

Soon after mating, the new queens fly off to find suitable locations for their winter sleep. The drones and the old queen die, leaving the leaderless colony in a state of unorganized chaos. Some of the workers even lay eggs, but their unfertilized efforts can only hatch into drones which are of no use to the dying colony. Others may turn to cannibalism and consume larvae left in the brood cells, a behavior that is unknown while the queen is alive.

By the time frost arrives in late fall the workers have died, leaving only the delicately molded paper nest as a mute monument to the once-thriving colony.

Hornet nests are not reused in subsequent years and are usually badly damaged or destroyed by winter storms. If you wish to collect one of these fascinating pieces of animal architecture, you should wait until after the first below-freezing night to be certain none of the occupants is still alive. Even a dying colony retains some of its instinct to protect its home and trying to collect a nest too soon could result in painful welts.

15

T he Fisher Rarely Fishes: Watching the nimble arboreal (relating to trees)
footwork of graceful little pine or Douglas squirrels, it is difficult to believe
these speedy climbers fear any four-footed predator. Yet, the Pine Marten, a
larger cousin of the slender weasel, regularly catches and eats these bushy-
tailed sprites in their own element — the tops of tall coniferous trees.

Astounding as this feat seems, it is dimmed by the ability of an even
larger member of the weasel tribe to catch and eat the Pine Marten. This
fox-sized hunter is the Fisher, *Martes pennanti*, a mysterious animal of the
deep woods, so secretive in its habits it is seldom seen, even by observant
naturalists searching for it.

Adult Fishers weigh from 6 to 12 pounds (2.7 to 5.4 kilograms), with
an occasional individual going a few pounds more. Most females weigh half
as much as the males. The rich fur of a Fisher is dark grayish-brown in
color, but may appear almost black in the dim light beneath the thick
forest canopy.

The Fisher's different silhouette makes it easy to tell it from the
similar-sized fox, even though both animals have long bushy tails. The
Fisher has the short, rounded ears of a weasel, barely projecting above the
soft fur of its head. In contrast, foxes (excepting the Arctic Fox) have erect,
pointed ears that are one of their most conspicuous features.

The Fisher has been described as a large black fox with the head of a
weasel. The 2½-inch-long (6.4-centimeter) paw tracks of a Fisher can
easily be distinguished from the dainty, four-toed print of a fox. The Fisher

leaves a five-toed track almost half again as big as those of the fox. Finding the track of a Fisher, however, can be very difficult as they often travel by jumping from tree to tree.

Fishers are poorly named. They seldom eat fish and there is little evidence they even catch the few fish they do consume. Their typical prey is small mammals and birds, such as squirrels, wood rats, marmots, quail, and grouse.

The Fisher is one of the few predators to regularly kill and eat porcupines. They don't always escape the sharp quills of these large rodents, for almost every Fisher examined has old quills lodged under its skin. But they do seem to be immune to the infections that plague other animals that run afoul of the well-armed quill pigs.

The luxurious fur of the Fisher is long and silky and very much in demand to satisfy the vanity of affluent women. Fishers were trapped and hunted almost to extinction in the 1920s and 1930s, but appear to be coming back after being afforded long-overdue legal protection.

Fishers have been reintroduced in parts of their former range where they had disappeared completely. One of the reasons for trying to reestablish Fishers is their ability to hold porcupine populations in check. Lumbermen dislike porcupines whose bark-feeding habits often result in misshapen trees less valuable as saw-logs.

Most recent sightings of Fishers in California have been in the dense forests of Bigfoot Country — in Humboldt, Trinity, Siskiyou, and Del Norte Counties. They also are known to occur in the Sierra, mainly in the region extending from Sequoia to Yosemite National Parks.

Many recent reports of these rare animals unfortunately have been of dead or dying Fishers taken from the deadly steel jaws of traps set for other animals. Trapping is a cruel and nonselective way of killing wildlife. Protected animals, such as the Fisher, River Otter, Pine Marten, and Ringtail will continue to die needlessly until this archaic practice has been abolished.

One interesting aspect of Fisher natural history is the reproductive cycle of the female. Once she reaches the breeding age of two years, she remains almost continuously pregnant for the rest of her life.

The gestation period of the Fisher is about 352 days, an extremely long time for such a small mammal. Shortly after giving birth in April, the female Fisher sneaks away from her new family and mates again. The newly formed embryos quickly go into a resting stage, development stopping completely until the following December.

This process, known as delayed implantation, is found in several

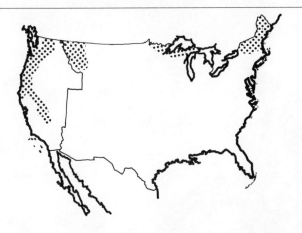

Fisher range

members of the weasel and bear families. Its significance is not completely clear, but biologists believe it allows both mating and birth to occur at a time of year when living conditions are most favorable in the harsh mountain environments inhabited by these animals.

Without delayed implantation, a Fisher mating in spring would give birth in winter — a time when finding food is difficult at best. Timing for a spring birth would require that adults mate in winter when all their energies are devoted to just surviving.

Newborn Fishers, called kits, are about four inches (10 centimeters) long and a typical litter numbers two or three. They are helpless until their eyes open at about seven weeks, then grow rapidly. They are ready to leave the den and learn to hunt with their mother by the end of their third month.

Fishers are solitary animals and the male takes no part in raising the young. The mother and her kits of the year part company in late fall. Each kit will seek out its own territory, which may cover 100 square-miles (260 square-kilometers).

Winter is a time of extreme hardship for the Fisher, as it is for other meat-eaters. Fishers don't hibernate, but remain active in the deep snows of the high mountains. Food is very scarce, for most of the birds have flown south and many small mammals are asleep in winter dens beneath the blanket of snow.

It is then that the porcupine, also a nonhibernator, becomes essential to the survival of the Fisher. It is not hard to understand how the Fisher got started on this hazardous eating habit.

The sapsucker drills holes in bark,
then laps up the sap.

16

It's Not Much of a Name: Although most bird names convey a fairly accurate description, some sound just a little bit ridiculous. One of these is the Yellow-bellied Sapsucker, *Syphrapicus varius*, a colorful woodpecker common throughout most of the United States.

The two species of sapsuckers in North America have evolved a novel method of obtaining a part of their diet with no competition from other birds. Just like humans who tap sugar maples to make syrup, these birds drill holes in the bark of trees and lap up the exuding sap with brush-like tongues.

Sapsuckers reap an additional food benefit from their bark drilling. The sweet drops of thick resin attract insects, which are desert for the birds when they make their periodic rounds of feeding stations.

Sapsuckers are small woodpeckers measuring only about eight inches (20 centimeters) in length. The yellow-bellied part of their common name actually applies to the Eastern race of the species. Western birds seldom show any yellow on the breast and are often called Red-breasted Sapsuckers.

The best field marks of the Western race are bright red head, throat, and upper breast and the large white shoulder patches on its black wings. The Williamson's Sapsucker, a bird of the higher mountains, shows similar white wing patches in the male but the only red is a small spot on the throat below the bill.

The favorite nesting habitats of Yellow-bellied Sapsuckers are lovely groves of Quaking Aspens along streams and near springs at the higher elevations of the Sierra and other Western ranges. Almost all of the nests I have found have been in living aspens and most have been quite close to the ground — they make ideal photographic subjects for the nest cavities are often drilled right at tripod height.

Aspens are probably chosen because they are so easy to hollow out. These relatively short-lived trees begin dying by becoming soft and pithy at the core while the outside still looks healthy. Often all a woodpecker has to do is drill through an inch or two of sound outer wood to get into softer material that can be quickly excavated for a nest.

The entrance to a sapsucker's nest is a nearly perfectly round hole about 1½ inches (4 centimeters) in diameter. The cavity itself is gourd-shaped, with the larger end placed downward and about 8 to 10 inches (20 to 25 centimeters) below the entrance. Some soft wood chips are left in the cavity to cushion the clutch of four to six white eggs that are laid soon after the completion of the nest.

I spent one Memorial Day weekend photographing sapsuckers and other cavity nesting birds in a small aspen grove in Nevada. The sapsuckers, the most numerous and conspicuous birds in the area, were in the process of constructing nesting cavities.

Many other species benefit from the cavity building activities of the sapsuckers. Some even try to take over before the sapsuckers have completed the nests and raised their own broods.

I had set up a remote-operated camera with a long lens only four feet from a new nest cavity being constructed by a pair of sapsuckers. Like all newlyweds, the couple frequently would take time out from their work to indulge in nuptial play. These pleasant interludes usually took place in another tree some distance from the nest.

As soon as the sapsuckers vacated the premises, a pair of diminutive House Wrens would move in and immediately begin carrying nesting material into the partially completed cavity. Upon the return of the rightful owners, the wrens would be quickly put to rout, but not without spending some time loudly proclaiming their squatter's rights by buzzy scolding from a nearby limb.

The sapsuckers would remove the furnishings brought in by the wrens and go back to their task of enlarging the cavity. The wrens continued in their attempts to take over the premises for the three days I spent there and I was able to take many photographs of both species using the same camera set-up.

I left before finding out who finally won that game of musical nests,

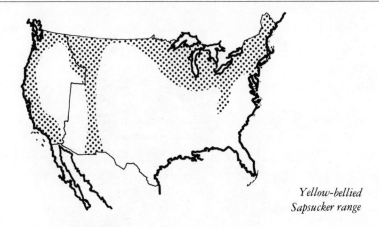

*Yellow-bellied
Sapsucker range*

but I was putting my money on the larger sapsuckers.

Sapsuckers seem to do the bulk of their bark-drilling while wintering at the lower elevations. The distinctive patterns left by their work, consisting of horizontal bands of tiny rectangular or round holes, can be seen on many different species of trees in the valleys and foothills. They return to the same trees year after year.

Some trees, such as the Blue Oaks, will produce distinctive thickening of the bark as scar tissue is formed to heal the wounds caused by the birds. The sapsuckers will then return and drill another row of holes along the center of the thickened ridge. After many years, the trunks of the trees may look like a huge lathe turning with symmetrical ridges perhaps six inches (15 centimeters) thick ringing it in many places.

Sapsuckers have often been blamed for killing trees with their bark drilling, but I have seen very little evidence of this. Most of the hole patterns I have observed seem to be spaced enough to leave some cambium (growing layer) untouched and thus the trees are not completely girdled.

It will boldly attack anything that threatens its nest.

17

T he Fearless Defender: To an ardent birder, the simultaneous discovery of two new birds is about on par with a golfer's hole-in-one. I've enjoyed this rare good luck on several occasions, but one such event in particular stands out as a highlight of my outdoor adventures.

I was hiking in the Montana Rockies northwest of Yellowstone National Park and had dropped my pack and leaned back against a friendly fir stump for a welcome morning break. As I gnawed on a salty chunk of beef jerky and sat reveling in the clear, cool air at 9,000 feet (2,700 meters) on the backbone of the continent, I observed a large bird in a clearing a few hundred feet below.

A quick look through binoculars confirmed what I already suspected. The chicken-like bird was a Spruce Grouse — a species which, until that moment, had successfully evaded all my attempts to add it to my life list of birds seen in the field.

My first Spruce Grouse was calmly feeding on the fruit of low-growing alpine blueberries just beginning to ripen in the chill of late September. It was a beautiful rooster, and I noted the bright red spot above the eye that makes it easy to separate from the larger Blue Grouse.

Suddenly, a feathered bolt of blue lightning flashed through the field of my binoculars. The fast-moving object arrowed toward the unsuspecting grouse which literally exploded in a puff of feathers. As the unbelievable scene came into sharp focus, a large blue-gray hawk mantled the dying grouse with spread wings, holding it to the ground with one great talon.

My own morning snack quickly forgotten, I spent the next hour watching my second life bird of the day. The Goshawk, *Accipiter gentilis*, carefully picked the feathers and then consumed most of the meat from a bird whose weight must have been half its own. Then, breakfast over, the great raptor flew with rapid wing beats to a sunny branch in a Douglas Fir. Here it spent another 20 minutes preening before again taking wing and disappearing into the green canopy of the thick boreal forest.

The Goshawk is the largest and rarest of North America's three species of forest hawks. Like the smaller Sharp-shinned and Cooper's Hawks, to which it is closely related, it has a long tail and short rounded wings beautifully adapted to the task of capturing avian prey in thick cover.

In the West, the Goshawk is found mostly at higher elevations in the dense coniferous forests of the Canadian Life Zone. During winter, migrants from the north may appear almost anywhere, but valley sightings are rare enough to cause some excitement in birding circles.

Goshawks build a large stick nest, usually placed well up in a tall conifer. It is most often located on a large horizontal limb near the trunk and from 30 to 50 feet (9 to 15 meters) above the ground.

The typical clutch of a Goshawk numbers three to five eggs and the incubation time is about 28 days. When hatched, Goshawk chicks are covered with short, silky down, white in color. This is soon replaced with longer, denser down of a darker shade of gray.

The only Goshawk nest I have ever been fortunate enough to find was in the spectacular Wind River Mountains of Wyoming. It was about 35 feet (11 meters) up in a large Douglas Fir on a steep, densely wooded slope. When I found the nest in late June it contained three half-grown young hawks whose flight feathers were just beginning to appear at the tips of their stubby wings.

Goshawks are extremely defensive of their nests and will boldly attack anything on two or four legs that approaches too closely. I learned how formidable they can be when I had been watching and photographing the Wind River nest for about two weeks. During my absence, a falconer — who was a student at Audubon Camp of the West where I was teaching for the summer — climbed the tree in an unfortunate attempt to steal the young birds.

Phyllis and I were headed for the same nest, and when we arrived at the tree it was occupied by one badly shaken young falconer. He was desperately trying to ward off attacks of the angry female Goshawk while working his way back down to the ground. The nestling hawks, almost ready to fledge, had abandoned the nest in panic. One had flown past us on

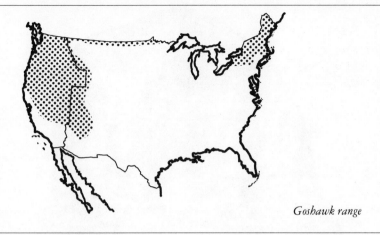

Goshawk range

wobbly wings as we scrambled up the steep slope laden down with photographic equipment.

Our arrival distracted the female and the culprit was able to make it safely to the ground while she directed her attacks at us. She had struck him repeatedly with open talons and had ripped the shirt off his back along with a little of his hide. He recovered, but whether the experience deterred him from future nest raids I do not know.

This type of nest vandalism is not an unusual occurrence. Their great speed and maneuverability, coupled with their ability to kill large prey, has made Goshawks a long-time favorite of falconers. This popularity, unfortunately, has contributed to the decline of the species. Falconers often destroy an entire year's nesting attempt by a breeding pair to obtain a single young hawk to train.

Whether falconry is a legitimate use of our dwindling population of raptorial birds is an oft-debated question. There is no doubt that certain species, such as the Red-tailed Hawk and the American Kestrel, still are common enough so their future is not, at least currently, threatened by falconry.

It is the rarest and most threatened of our hawks — such as the Peregrine Falcon and Goshawk — that are most in demand by falconers. Even though they are protected from being taken for falconry in many states, there is a lucrative black market in these species. Many are transported across state lines to areas where they cannot be obtained from wild populations. This unnecessary drain could well push an endangered species into extinction.

The Spotted Owl is seldom seen.

18

An Owl Takes a Bow: My most exciting encounters with wildlife take place when I least expect them. Such was the case when I saw and photographed my first Spotted Owl, *Strix occidentalis*, in the Sierra Nevada. This tame but usually very secretive creature is one of the most difficult to find of all Western owls.

Phyllis and I had driven into the Sierra, east of Nevada City, California, to scout a field trip for a natural history class I was to teach several weeks later. We were driving at a snail's pace along a U.S. Forest Service road, searching the shaded bank on the uphill side for Lady's-slipper Orchids we had found there the previous year.

As we rounded a turn in the road, I glanced upward into the green canopy above. There, in a small Pacific Dogwood tree, a large bird perched almost over the road. From its big-headed and short-tailed silhouette, it was obviously an owl. Its mottled brown color and lack of ear-tufts immediately identified it as the Spotted Owl, the rare Western counterpart of the Barred Owl of the East.

I stopped the van almost under the sleepy bird and we glassed it through the windshield, expecting it to fly at any instant.

When our big-eyed friend showed no evidence of taking flight, our thoughts turned to photographs. The gunstock-mounted cameras with long telephotos that laid on the back seat, ready for instant use, would have been of little value in that situation — the light level was too low and they couldn't be focused at so short a distance.

With fumbly fingers I quickly mounted an electronic flash unit on a camera equipped with a zoom lens and slipped out the door as quietly as possible. When I focused on the subject, a glance at the distance scale told me it was only 12 feet (3.7 meters) from the camera. I adjusted the diaphragm for this flash-to-subject distance and started exposing film as fast as my flash unit would recycle.

By the time I was ready to change film, Phyllis had her flash equipment assembled and it began to look like the Fourth of July had arrived early that year. The owl calmly followed us with its gaze by twisting its neck. It never flinched at the barrage of light.

When we had taken about 40 exposures, I climbed onto the roof of the van for even closer pictures. Now I was shooting from only eight feet (2.4 meters), holding the camera to fill the frame with a vertical format. I didn't stop taking pictures until the slow recycling time told me my strobe batteries were exhausted.

Satisfied we had good photographs, we bid our friend goodbye and drove on, still tingling from the excitement of our rare find. Just locating a Spotted Owl high in a dense conifer would have been a fortunate discovery — finding one perched near the ground in an open tree was almost more than any nature photographer could hope for.

When we returned several hours later, the owl still was perched in the same spot. We worried about its obvious location with weekend hunters driving the backroads and decided to try to flush it to a more concealed roosting spot.

I walked directly under the bird and clapped my hands, expecting to see it spread its great wings and fly silently away. It just blinked its dime-sized brown eyes and looked down at me. I felt it was saying, "What are those fools up to now?"

When clapping and shouting proved ineffective, we tried sounding the horn. Still the owl sat and calmly watched us. Finally, in desperation, I climbed the steep bank and shook the small tree in which it perched.

This indignity was too much for even a friendly Spotted Owl. It uttered a soft *"whoo-whoo"* and flew across the road to perch near the trunk of a large Douglas Fir. Here its cryptic (concealing) coloration rendered it almost invisible. Had we not known it was there we would not have been able to see it from the road.

In the '70's, the California Department of Fish and Game conducted a study to determine the status of the Spotted Owl. The owls were located by using recorded or vocal calls along roads and trails in areas of typical habitat and listening for answers.

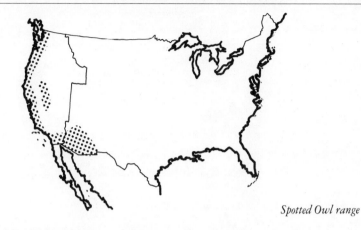

Spotted Owl range

The study found Spotted Owls in at least 33 California counties. The highest population densities were in the Douglas Fir belt of the North Coast region and in mixed coniferous forests on the western slope of the Southern Sierra. The study located 263 individual Spotted Owls, which were considered to represent 192 pairs of the birds.

In comparing the results of this study with known past locations, a 27 percent reduction was noted. This might indicate a downward trend in the California population of Spotted Owls.

One interesting result was sightings in El Dorado, Nevada, Yuba, Sierra, and Plumas Counties. There had been no previous reports from any of these.

According to DFG's study, the most important habitat requirement for Spotted Owls is dense coniferous forest. They may disappear completely from heavily logged areas and are much less common in areas where logging occurs than in parks or other protected areas where logging is not permitted.

This clearly points out the need to leave intact large blocks of timber to satisfy the needs of forest-loving animals such as the Spotted Owl. It is true that trees do come back after being cut, but it may take scores or hundreds of years to reestablish wildlife and plant communities that proliferated prior to the devastation created by clear-cut logging.

Vicious battles sometimes end in the death of one of the gladiators.

19

T urkeys Are Spectacular Birds:
Few sights in nature can match the strut-
ting dance of a Wild Turkey tom, performed during the mating rites of
spring. Weighing up to 25 pounds (11 kilograms), gobblers look still
larger with their tails spread into a perfect fan, their wings drooped to
almost drag the ground, and their bronzed plumage ruffled in full display
posture.

The spectacle of Wild Turkeys, *Meleagris gallopavo*, is a relatively new
treat for Californians, for this species is not a native. Because of their wary
nature and savory meat, they have been introduced as a game species and
now occur in huntable numbers in at least 24 of California's counties.

When the pilgrims first arrived in New England, they found the
woodlands teeming with these big birds which quickly became an
important source of protein. However, uncontrolled hunting and the rapid
destruction of the bird's habitat took a heavy toll. By the end of the last
century, Wild Turkeys were considered prime candidates for early
extinction.

The Wild Turkey, which was first runner-up for the rank of our
national bird, was saved by the enactment of game laws to control the
number killed by hunters. Now, after nearly a century of careful
management and restocking, a nationwide population of about 1.5 million
birds is spread over at least 43 states, including several, such as California,
which had no Wild Turkeys before.

Tom Turkeys spend the winter in bachelor flocks that amicably forage and roost together, with no hint of the fierce battles to be fought in spring. Triggered by the increasing day length of late January and February, these all-male groups begin to break up and each tom seeks out a territory of four to eight acres from which he will attempt to exclude all males of his species.

The dominant males gather on a strutting ground where they gobble and dance under the admiring gaze of the local hen population. A successful tom may gather a harem of five hens which he will defend with beak and spurs against competitors. Vicious battles have been known to end in death.

After a hen has chosen a tom, she will mate only with him and will nest within the territory he defends. Frequent mating takes place until the hen completes her clutch of 8 to 15 eggs and begins incubating them. At that time she completely ignores her pompous lord and master. There is an oft-repeated but unconfirmed story that tom Turkeys will purposely destroy a clutch of eggs if they find them, in order to prolong the mating season.

Hen Turkeys are tight sitters and can often be approached closely without their leaving the nest. The longer a hen incubates her eggs, the more attached she becomes to them and the less likely she is to abandon them if disturbed. Incubation takes four weeks and all the young hatch within a very brief time interval.

Young Turkey poults are precocial and leave the nest soon after hatching. In a short time they are following the mother about in search of insects, which they find for themselves. Although Turkeys feed mostly on seeds and acorns as adults, the poults must have animal protein to put on the large amount of body weight they gain in the first few months.

Although they are sought by numerous predators, rain seems to pose the greatest danger to young Turkeys in the first few weeks of their lives. Unlike young ducklings, their down is not waterproof and they usually will die after a thorough soaking. Heavy spring rains always have a devastating impact on the reproductive success of Wild Turkeys.

Most of the growth energy during early life goes to produce primary wing-feathers and strong flight muscles. By the time Turkey poults are two weeks old they can fly up into a tree to escape ground-prowling enemies. This is a common trait among the gallinaceous birds (quail, pheasant, grouse, and Turkey). Among most other birds, the young are unable to fly until body weight and size reaches adult proportions.

The wing span of adult Wild Turkeys is only slightly more than four feet (1.2 meters), a size that would seem much too small to lift their great

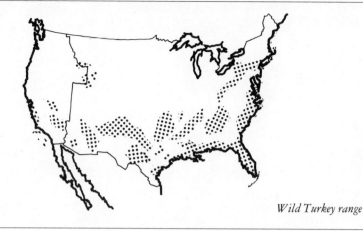

Wild Turkey range

bulk. Part of the answer to this seeming disregard for the laws of aerodynamics lies in the shape of the wings. Some of what they lack in span is made up in chord — the front-to-back dimension of the wing. Thus, due to a large chordal distance, the wings of a Wild Turkey may have two or three times the wing area of another bird that measures the same span. The balance of their wing inadequacy is compensated by tremendous breast muscles which beat the wings at a relatively rapid rate for such a large bird. Turkeys have been clocked at close to 60 miles (97 kilometers) per hour.

One of Nature's truly soul-stirring spectacles is a flock of wild gobblers leaving the roost in a tall tree and taking wing against the rosy glow of a dawn sky. From high on a ridge top they launch their great bodies, fly rapidly for several hundred feet, and then set their wings for a long sloping glide to feeding grounds in a canyon far below. I have witnessed this on several occasions and it left me longing for a repeat performance.

20

A Little Bird With Its Own Style: A characteristic sound of the deciduous woodlands of the West is a nasal *"quaank, quaank, quaank"* that reminds me of the horn of some diminutive foreign-made automobile. This is the distinctive call of the White-breasted Nuthatch, *Sitta carolinensis*, a strange little bird with eccentric habits almost as unusual as its name.

Contrary to common belief, the name nuthatch does not mean it wastes its time trying to incubate acorns. The "hatch" is archaic English for "hack" and refers to its method of feeding on nuts. These are often wedged into a crack in tree bark and given repeated sharp blows with the bird's slender bill until they are reduced to bite-sized kernels.

The White-breasted Nuthatch resembles a miniature woodpecker. Both woodpeckers and nuthatches feed on insects on the bark of trees but in a different manner. A woodpecker props itself upright, using its strong feet and stiff, pointed tail as the three legs of a tripod. Nuthatches feed head downward, hanging by their toenails from the cracks and crevices in the bark.

The White-breasted Nuthatch can be easily separated from the Brown Creeper, another bark-probing bird of similar size, by its eating habits. Creepers fly to the base of a tree, then work their way upwards, probing for insect larvae and pupae with their slender, downward-curving bills. In contrast, nuthatches fly to the top of a tree and work their way down, using their slightly upturned bills to make the bark chips fly as they energetically forage.

91

The White-breasted Nuthatch is a tiny, sparrow-sized bird with plumage of contrasting shades of white, black, and gray. The male has a black cap and nape (back of the neck); the female's cap and nape are a shade of gray darker than her blue-gray wings and back. The contrasting dark and light patterns on the tail show well when either bird takes wing.

Nuthatches nest in old woodpecker holes or in natural cavities in trees. They don't seem to be too particular about height for I have found their nests as low as eye-level in a Blue Oak trunk, to as high as 60 feet (18 meters) up in a branch of a huge Valley Oak. The entrance hole is often in the bottom side of a large horizontal limb.

Nuthatches often line the bottom of their nesting cavity with several inches of assorted materials. Tree bark and animal hair seem to be most commonly used. I've watched nuthatches bring lichen-covered slabs of bark as big as themselves to the nest, and then be unable to wedge them in through the tiny opening.

The mammal hair used by nuthatches as a final cushion for their eggs is usually obtained by pulling it out of a dead animal. I've watched them pull great tufts of fur from a very ripe ground-squirrel carcass and carry it back to the nest. This habit often makes a nuthatch nest smell more like a vulture's aerie than a tidy songbird's domicile.

Large families are typical of the White-breasted Nuthatch and the hen will lay from five to ten — most frequently eight — eggs in the newly lined nest. Both parents share in the incubation, which usually takes 12 days. When the nestlings hatch, both parent birds are busy from dawn to dusk hunting protein-rich insect food for all those hungry mouths.

When the young nuthatches leave the nest cavity for the first time, they are unable to fly but can scamper about on the bark almost as nimbly as their parents. Their first plumage is almost identical to that of adults.

The parents continue to feed young nuthatches for about two weeks after they leave the nest. By then the youngsters have learned to find insects for themselves and become independent individuals. They apparently do not re-enter the nest for nighttime shelter during this period, but roost hanging upside-down from a branch of the nest tree.

White-breasted Nuthatches are found mostly in deciduous woodland in the valleys and foothills. They are not migratory, but seem to wander up to higher elevations in late summer after completion of their nesting chores. At this time they may occur in the same area as the Red-breasted and Pygmy Nuthatches of the coniferous forests.

During winter, White-breasted Nuthatches easily can be attracted to suet in bird feeders. This should be attached to a tree trunk or feeder by

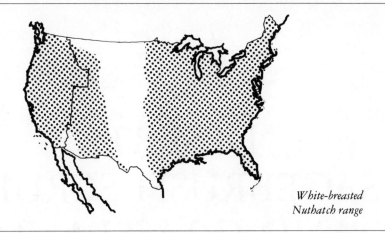

*White-breasted
Nuthatch range*

nailing a piece of hardware cloth over it to keep jays and other larger birds from flying off with it.

White-breasted Nuthatches occasionally will nest in a birdhouse, although they seem to prefer natural or woodpecker-made cavities. Natural looking birdhouses can be made by splitting a short length of tree limb lengthwise and hollowing out the center of both halves with mallet and chisel. Drill an entrance hole of the proper size (about 1¼ inch — 32 millimeters — in diameter for nuthatches) in one of the halves so it intersects the cavity at one end. Then reassemble the two halves by wiring, nailing, or gluing them back together. The entrance hole should be about 6 inches (15.2 centimeters) above the floor of the nest to allow room for lining material.

Part Two

DESERT, SAGEBRUSH SCRUB, AND GRASSLAND

The Easterner traveling for the first time in the West is likely to be awestruck by the vast open vistas. Lacking sufficient rainfall to support the woodlands and forests found in the East, the valleys, plains, and plateaus of the West offer little to block the view of distant mountains.

Although it is an oversimplification, we can classify the natural plant communities of the open Western countryside as either desert, sagebrush scrub, or grassland. Many ecological factors combine and interact to determine which of these three will dominate in a given area but the amount and pattern of the annual precipitation is by far the most important.

True deserts, such as California's Mojave and Arizona's Sonora, receive less than ten inches of rainfall each year and this occurs in a rather irregular pattern. Some desert areas may go for several years with no measurable precipitation.

Both the plants and the animals of the desert have learned to live with short water rations. Some animals, such as the nocturnal Kangaroo Rats, can live entirely on the water produced by their own metabolism. The Desert Tortoise solves its water problems much like a camel — it drinks a lot of water when it finds a source, storing the surplus under its shell. When water is not available, it can live by eating succulent desert cacti. The venomous scorpion avoids fatal dessication by venturing forth only during the cool of the desert night.

Fish may seem unlikely members of desert fauna. However, several species of colorful little pupfish, relics of a bygone time when water was more plentiful, have sought a last refuge in a few scattered desert streams and hot springs. Most are endangered species due to the fragile nature of their tiny habitats.

A single species of plant, Great Basin Sagebrush, dominates millions of acres of Western flat lands. This sagebrush scrub is home to the fleetfooted Pronghorn, often called antelope although it really belongs to a family all its own with no other living close relatives. Sharing the sagebrush with the Pronghorn is the Sage Grouse, the largest grouse in North America and famous for the dawn dances performed on special strutting grounds by the males.

In summer, the characteristic sound of the sagebrush country is the monotonous buzz of cicadas. These large insects, relatives of the aphids and leaf hoppers, spend the vast majority of their lives underground. They emerge in spring and summer as flying adults and live only long enough to mate and reproduce.

Western grasslands are home to the long-eared Black-tailed Jackrabbit and the sweet singing Western Meadowlark. Gophersnakes prowl in search of rodent prey like the vole, a fat meadowmouse whose presence is known by the neat hidden runways it constructs in the matted grass.

Any skunk wandering about in the daytime should be avoided.

21

W oods Pussy Has Few Enemies:
The Striped Skunk, *Mephitis mephitis,* is
one of the least wary of all of our Western mammals. When it encounters a
human or other predator, it usually just goes about its business unless the
intruder approaches too closely. Then, instead of running away, it will give
several warning signals and, if still harassed, will finally resort to its
ultimate weapon of defense.

The Striped Skunk belongs to a worldwide family of carnivores called
the Mustelidae. This group, which includes Badgers, weasels, Wolverines,
and others, is named for the highly developed anal musk glands in its
members. However, while most of the relatives use these scent glands only
for social communication, those of the skunk have evolved into very
effective chemical defense weapons.

If approached too closely, a Striped Skunk may show it is annoyed by
stamping its front feet on the ground and may also hiss and growl. This is
usually enough to cause most enlightened people or predators to detour,
giving the little black-and-white woods pussy as much of the trail as it
desires.

If this subtle hint does not suffice, a skunk next will turn its rump
toward its tormentor and elevate its plume-like black-and-white tail. Each
long and coarse hair on this beautiful brush stands at right angles and the
house-cat-sized animal suddenly appears about twice as large as it really is.

Even with tail elevated, a skunk usually holds its fire until actually
attacked. It may instinctively realize it has a limited amount of

97

ammunition and doesn't waste any while the enemy is out of range.

The skunk has two musk glands, located on either side of the anal opening. Each gland has a protrudable nozzle and the discharge force is produced by large muscles in the hips. The effective range is about 10 feet (3 meters) , but may be greater in a downwind direction.

If finally provoked into spraying, a skunk will deliver, with a surprising degree of accuracy, a small quantity of an acrid yellow liquid. It has somewhat the same effect as teargas. Dogs that have caught a well-directed charge will roll on the ground, wipe their muzzles in the dirt, and sometimes vomit. If the spray hits the eyes, it causes severe burning and watering, but will not cause blindness as some people believe.

The most obvious characteristics of skunk musk are its intense odor and its great persistence. Clothing that has been sprayed will continue to smell for weeks or months — even after the odor appears to have dissipated, a wetting will bring it back.

Skunks are nocturnal animals, seldom encountered abroad in daylight. In fact, any skunk seen wandering about much after dawn or very long before dusk should be avoided because of the danger of its being rabid. Rabies is endemic in many skunk populations and, while few people are ever bitten, skunks that are behaving abnormally should be given a wide berth.

Striped Skunks are omnivorous, meaning they feed on both plant and animal material. During spring and summer, insects seem to make up a great deal of their diet. A foraging skunk will dig many shallow holes seeking burrowing insects it locates by its well-developed sense of smell.

Mice, gophers, and other small rodents often are captured and the eggs and young of ground-nesting birds are eaten at times. Skunks are not climbers, so any bird that nests above the ground is safe from them.

Skunks eat the fruits of many wild and domestic plants. They are not above eating carrion, and many are hit by vehicles while feeding on road-kills on the highway.

Striped Skunks are found throughout the United States as well as in Canada and Mexico. The intensive settlement of the North American continent has increased the edge type of habitat favored by skunks and they are probably more numerous now than they were in pristine (earliest) times. Three other species, Spotted, Hooded, and Hog-nosed Skunks are found within the United States.

Striped Skunks are relatively prolific. A single litter of 4 to 9 is born in early May. They come into the world naked, blind, earless, and toothless and spend the first two months of their lives in a snug underground den.

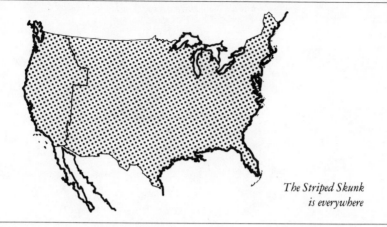

The Striped Skunk
is everywhere

After this, they are able to follow their mother about on her nightly forays.

Skunks are not true hibernators, but they may sleep during much of the winter in colder climates. They often sleep in communal dens and as many as 15 have been found cuddled up to take advantage of each other's body heat.

Unfortunately, skunks show little fear of traps and each winter many are killed in this way for their pelts. The skins, however, have little value and usually are used to trim inexpensive coats. Trappers receive about $2.50 for any average pelt in the West. It is hardly enough to compensate trappers for the very real danger of contracting rabies through a cut in the skin while skinning their victims.

Young skunks are attractive animals and a natural reaction is to want to take one home for a pet. They can be deodorized by a veterinarian, and will become quite docile, but pet skunks are illegal in many areas because of the danger of rabies.

Although humans kill them in large numbers, their effective defense system results in skunks having very few natural enemies. Bobcats, Coyotes, foxes, and other large mammalian predators may take them when other food is scarce, but don't make a normal practice of dining on skunk.

One predator that appears to like skunk flesh is the Great Horned Owl. This fierce, winged tiger-of-the-night, like most birds, has a very poorly developed sense of smell and seems little affected by a dose of skunk musk. As an added protection, the owl has a transparent third eyelid, called the nictitating membrane, that can be closed without affecting its vision.

I have found skunk remains around the nests of Great Horned Owls and every adult I have ever examined had an easily detected odor of skunk on its plumage.

*Young Barn Swallows remain in the nest for
three weeks.*

22

Thible to adapt to changes in its environment. Those that adapt continue
to exist and pass on useful adaptations to their progeny. Those that fail to
adapt simply become extinct.

Because humans have modified the natural environment at an
extremely accelerated rate in the last few centuries, they have increased the
rate of extinction. At the same time, certain species have taken advantage
of human modifications and have become more numerous.

Many birds have learned to use human structures to support and
shelter their nests. This relatively new nesting behavior is so commonplace
in some species that it is reflected in their vernacular names — Barn Owl,
House Wren, House Finch, and House Sparrow are a few examples.

The swallow family has several species that nest on human structures
and one of the best-known and loved is the beautiful Barn Swallow,
Hirundo rustica. The graceful aerobatics and cheerful twittering of these
aerial insectivores are familiar across rural North America.

Although named for their use of barn rafters as nest sites, they also
utilize many other structures such as bridges, unoccupied houses, garages,
boat docks, covered water tanks, and culverts to construct their beautifully
engineered nests of mud and straw. In primitive times, Barn Swallows
nested in caves and in rock crevices on cliff faces, and many still do.

Barn Swallows are the easiest to recognize of any of the members of
their clan. They are our only swallows with deeply forked tails, a field

mark that can be seen from some distance without binoculars. Their iridescent purple upper parts combined with rusty forehead, throat, and breast are also marks of distinction among their family members.

Immature Barn Swallows have sharply notched tails but lack the long, slender, outer tail feathers which produce the deep fork of the adults. The breast feathers of young birds are buff instead of rust colored and their backs and wings lack the beautiful iridescence of their elders. Both adults and immatures show white rectangular spots near the tips of their outer tail feathers when they spread these lovely fans in flight.

The entire swallow family, known scientifically as the Hirundinidae (hirundo is Latin and means a swallow), feeds almost entirely by capturing insects in flight. Because flying insects are scarce or absent during winter in temperate or arctic regions, swallows migrate to the tropics during such times and return north to breed in spring and summer.

The northward movement of swallows is closely timed to match the emergence of flying insects in spring. Unfortunately, their timing is too close in some years when unseasonably cold or wet weather lasts well into spring. Deprived of their only means of obtaining fuel for their tiny feathered bodies, millions may starve to death. However, they are prolific breeders and one successful nesting season can erase the losses of a migration disaster.

Although Barn Swallows are normally colonial nesters like many of their kin, some pairs seem to prefer privacy and solitude. It is not unusual to find only a single nesting pair in a small barn or outbuilding.

Both male and female work on the nest construction, a task that may take a week or more to complete. The nest begins as a circular plaque of mud plastered on a rough surface, often vertical but sometimes flat, to which small pellets of mud are attached, eventually forming a cup-like nest. Generous amounts of grass reinforce the masonry and the finished nest is a surprisingly sturdy structure. The final lining is of feathers and they seem to have a preference for those from white chickens.

Both parents take turns incubating the clutch of 4 to 6 brown-spotted white eggs. During the day the parents change places as often as every 10 minutes. The bird coming on duty will twitter softly while flying toward the nest and it seems as if it intends to land directly atop its incubating mate. At the last instant the setting bird takes flight and the fragile eggs are exposed only for a fraction of a second before again being protectively covered. At night the female does all of the incubating while the male watches over her from a nearby perch.

Young Barn Swallows remain in the nest for a relatively long time —

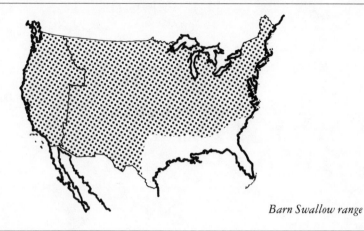

Barn Swallow range

up to three weeks. During this period the adults are kept busy from dawn to dark bringing countless thousands of insects to their hungry brood. A large family seems to more than fill the tiny nest as they grow and it appears some will certainly be crowded out by siblings. However, surprisingly few fall from the nest before taking their fledging flights.

In the more temperate parts of their vast breeding range, Barn Swallows often raise two broods per season. A number of observers have noted that Barn Swallow pairs that return to repair an old nest from the previous year usually raise two broods in it, while those that build a new nest usually raise but a single brood.

At the close of the nesting season, Barn Swallows gather in large flocks in preparation for their southward migration. These groups may number many thousands and be composed of other species of swallows as well. They often perch on power lines and are so evenly spaced along the wires that the gaps appear to be measured.

In the West, the first Barn Swallows arrive about March 1, and the last of the vast contingent departs by early November. Their winter range is in South America, requiring an annual flight of thousands of miles.

Alexander Wilson, the famous early American naturalist, made some calculations on how far a Barn Swallow might fly during a lifetime. He assumed an average speed of 60 miles (97 kilometers) per hour for 10 hours per day over a life span of 10 years. This totaled 2.2 million miles (3.52 million kilometers) or about 87 times around the earth — a distance that few jet-set humans equal in much longer lifetimes.

23

T he Endangered Fish of Death
Valley: Death Valley is an unlikely place to
look for fish. The meager surface water in this sun-baked desert has a
salinity several times that of the sea, may be almost hot enough to boil
eggs in summer, and has a dissolved-oxygen content that is barely
measurable. All these environmental conditions would be instantly lethal
to most fish.

Yet, the stinking saline hot springs and alkali marshes of this beautiful
but foreboding national monument contain several species of gutsy little
fish known collectively as Death Valley pupfish. These beautifully adapted
little finsters received their common name from ichthyologist Carl Hubbs,
who was fascinated by their almost puppy-like playful behavior.

Pupfish are thought to be relics of a bygone era when the Southwestern
deserts were far less arid than they are now. Vast lakes have since dried up,
leaving only simmering salt flats as testimony of their former grandeur.
Isolated populations of these hardy creatures sought refuge in tiny hot
springs, salt marshes, and meandering desert streams where they have
existed in precariously small numbers for thousands of years.

Pupfish belong to the worldwide killifish family, known scientifically
as the Cyprinodontidae. So tiny that they are often eaten by predaceous
diving beetles, these colorful animals have discovered a somewhat unique
way to avoid competition with larger fish — they live in water too hot and
too salty for most potential competitors.

During the Pleistocene Ice Age, the area now covered by Death Valley

A fish that lives in desert hot springs.

and much of the Mojave Desert contained large shallow lakes with interconnecting stream systems. The ancestors of the pupfish probably swam in the waters of this entire basin in conditions far less harsh than those of today.

Then, as the World's climate warmed up and the glaciers retreated, these lakes began to dry up. As they did, the waters became warmer and saltier at a rate far too rapid for most fish to adapt. Only the pupfish were able to change their physiology by evolution fast enough to survive the rapid shrinking of their watery habitat.

Each population of pupfish that was isolated from others of its own kind adapted to those particular conditions of its exile. So rapid were these adaptations that new species and subspecies were created in extremely short periods of evolutionary time.

Some pupfish have adapted to a wide range of water temperatures. During summer their tiny and shallow refuges are heated unmercifully by the desert sun. In winter, the same waters almost freeze as they radiate their energy into the vast heat sink of space through a cloudless desert sky.

Other pupfish live in hot springs that never vary more than a degree or two in temperature. One species lives in water at 112 degrees Fahrenheit (44.4 degrees Celsius) far too hot to support most forms of vertebrate life. Another pupfish has adapted to water six times as salty as that of the oceans. Under these conditions, typical saltwater fish such as herring and cod would quickly turn belly-up and die.

Pupfish have solved their food problems by adapting to a diet of plentiful algae. Because animal life of any kind is scarce, predaceous fish would find it difficult to make a living in desert hot springs. Algae, however, do very well in hot, salty water and provide a bountiful harvest for these little finny grazers.

It would seem that pupfish would be in little danger of extinction compared to other wildlife whose habitat is more sought after by humans and other animals. Unfortunately this is not the case. At least three types of pupfish once found in Death Valley have become extinct in recent years and several others are now on the list of threatened wildlife.

A number of factors, most of them man-caused, are to blame for the recent decline of desert pupfish. One important cause has been the introduction of predatory and competitive forms of fish. Exotics such as Mosquitofish, Goldfish, and Black Bass have been purposefully released into the fragile habitats of pupfish with disastrous results. One short-lived commercial venture utilized a desert hot spring as a hatchery for tropical aquarium fish — the effects on the native fish fauna (animal life) were catastrophic.

The clearing and leveling of desert land around hot springs has destroyed rare pupfish habitat. So tiny and fragile are many of these microenvironments that a shovelful of misplaced soil can do irreparable damage.

The Devil's Hole Pupfish, *Cyprinodon diabolis*, is confined to a single feeding ledge in a spring-fed pool in Ash Meadow, just east of Death Valley. The pumping of irrigation water from the aquifer (water-bearing stratum) that feeds this spring has threatened this species which ranges from as few as 125 breeding adults to a total of 800 individuals.

To protect the Devil's Hole Pupfish, 40 acres (16.1 hectares) were set aside as a detached section of Death Valley National Monument in 1952. In 1970, an artificial spawning platform was added to replace the natural

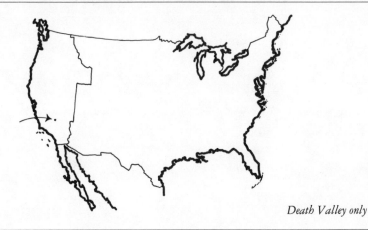

Death Valley only

spawning ledge that had become exposed by the lowered water table.
Despite these protective measures, the Devil's Hole Pupfish is doomed to
extinction if its home spring is pumped dry by the marginal agricultural
endeavors in the surrounding desert.

The Amargosa Pupfish, *Cyprinodon nevadensis*, has the widest range of
any Death Valley pupfish. Six separate subspecies are found at various
locations in the Armagosa River basin, a stream system which drains into
the valley from the south. One, the Tecopa Pupfish, was eliminated from
its home in Tecopa Spring by the introduction of Mosquitofish and human
contamination of the water.

The Salt Creek Pupfish, *Cyprinodon salinus*, has a home range extending
along two miles of Salt Creek. Because of its more extensive habitat, this
species has avoided the rare or endangered lists.

In contrast, the Cottonball Marsh Pupfish, *Cyprinodon milleri*, is found
in a single marsh near the sink of Salt Creek. Although its population was
considered stable in 1979, it is included on the rare list in California
because it could easily be decimated by any degradation of its fragile
habitat.

Protecting rare or endangered species is costly. The entire program
often is criticized by those who feel we have little to gain by saving obscure
species of tiny fish in a desert hot spring. But there are several good reasons
for saving the pupfish:

First, humankind has a moral obligation to prevent the extinction of
any species, especially when that extinction would result from the selfish
and thoughtless acts of people.

Secondly, and in a more practical vein, we can learn a lot studying an
organism that has adapted to life in desert hot springs and alkali pools.

Perhaps it was put together with left over parts.

24

The Coatis Semaphore: The Coati, *Nasua narica*, is a rough-and-tumble border ruffian that barely qualifies as a U.S. inhabitant. It seems to be put together from leftover parts, with the tail of a spider monkey, the muzzle of an anteater, the claws of a badger, the canine teeth of a Coyote, the flat-footed gait of a bear, and the unmitigated spunk of a Wolverine.

The Coati — its full name is Coatimundi — belongs to a small family of carnivores called the Procyonidae that includes only three other New World members. These are the Raccoon, the Ringtail, and the Kinkajou. It shares its rather abbreviated U.S. range with the Raccoon and Ringtail, but the Kinkajou is found only south of the border.

Although the Coati weighs roughly the same as the Raccoon, it is a rangier looking animal and, with its tapering two-foot (61-centimeter) tail, may reach a length of more than four feet (1.2 meters). Its tail is often carried straight up in the air and when a tribe of Coatis are foraging in low vegetation, waving tails are usually the first indication of their presence.

Perhaps the most striking physical characteristic of the Coati is its slender anteater-like muzzle. This is tipped with a tough, upturned snout that tapers to a point to make a perfect digging and probing instrument.

Like the Raccoon, the Coati has a mask-like pattern around its dark eyes, but the pattern is reversed on the Coati. It shows a light-colored mask against a dark background.

The Coati's magnificent tail shows dark rings like that of the Raccoon, but these may be so faded on older individuals that they are all but

109

invisible. The coarse pelage (hair covering) of a Coati is a uniform brown, but varies a great deal in shade from one region to another. There is even a good deal of color variation among individuals of the same tribe.

The main stronghold of the Coati is in the American tropics from northern Mexico to Argentina. It has extended its range northward into the United States in relatively recent times, possibly within the last century. It has been reported in the border regions of Texas, New Mexico, and Arizona, but only Arizona has a firmly established population of any size. Author-naturalist Bil Gilbert, who has done the most extensive field study of the Coati in Arizona, estimates the population fluctuates between 500 and 1,500 individuals.

Coatis are known to the prospectors and cowpunchers of the border country as chulo bears or Mexican monkeys. Many myths and tales have evolved about these mystery animals and some at least have a basis in fact.

One tall tale which is pure myth is that they can hang from a tree by their long tails and slash pursuing hounds to ribbons with their sharp claws. They certainly can do a job on any hound foolish enough to chase them, but they are not able to hang by their tails. Unlike the Spider Monkey's similar appendage, the Coati's tail is not prehensile (adapted for grasping). Coatis are, however, very adept climbers and use their tails for balance as they leap from one tree to another in monkey fashion.

Bil Gilbert discovered that a Coati tribe is an intricately organized social group which communicates by means of a vocal language of squeals, chirps, and grunts.

In addition, Gilbert found the Coati uses its tail for visual communication — as a sort of semaphore. When a member of a foraging tribe finds food, its tail vibrates excitedly as a signal to other members. Perhaps this accounts for the unusual manner in which Coatis carry their tails high overhead when searching for food.

The Arizona Coatis are found in four mountain ranges that extend across the international border and rise like cool islands above the scorching Sonoran desert. The Baboquivaris, the Santa Ritas, the Huachucas, and the Chiricahuas — even their Spanish and Indian names carry an air of mystery — are known to most naturalists as the Mexican Mountains. These wildly beautiful ranges are the northernmost home of many species of Mexican animals in addition to the Coati.

The Coppery-tailed Trogon (now called the Elegant Trogon), a smaller relative of the Resplendent Quetzal, nests in small numbers in several of these ranges and each year thousands of birders travel in hopes of adding it to their life lists.

Coati range

It was on such a trip that I saw my first Coati. Having had no luck in our first day's search for the elusive Trogon, we hiked up a steep-walled canyon in the Santa Ritas after dark in search of another border rarity, the Whiskered Owl. This Mexican species so closely resembles our common Screech Owl that the two cannot be separated in the field except by differences in their calls.

Quite by accident we located an owl's nest in the top of a broken-off snag and watched the adults feed the nearly fledged owlets in the beams of our flashlights. They were either Whiskered or Screech Owls, but they wouldn't call while near the nest so we couldn't identify them.

With ears tuned to the soft night sounds around us, we picked up the rhythmic crunching of oak leaves as what seemed to be a large animal walked down the canyon toward us. With thoughts of many exciting possibilities, we switched off our lights and waited in the moonless Arizona night. When the shuffling sounds seemed only yards away, we stabbed the darkness with twin beams of light to reveal a very surprised Coati out for an evening stroll.

It isn't unusual for a Coati to be seen in the Santa Ritas. It is unusual, however, for a single Coati to be out after dark. These highly social animals do most of their foraging between dawn and dusk and in the company of 15 to 40 tribe members. Since then I have read that some cantankerous old males are quite solitary, and that was probably what we observed that memorable night in the Santa Ritas.

*A Sage Grouse rooster produces low, staccato grunts,
intermingled with loud purring.*

25

Dawn Dancers of the Sagebrush Country: Nature has evolved many strange and bizarre forms of mating behavior that help assure only the most fit males pass on their genes to future generations. One of the strangest of these is known as arena behavior, in which the males defend mating stations that are unrelated to either feeding or nesting activities.

Of the one million or more animal species that inhabit the earth, less than one hundred are known to indulge in arena behavior. In the West, our most famous arena species is the Sage Grouse, *Centrocercus urophasianus*, North America's largest grouse and second in size only to the Wild Turkey among our gallinaceous birds.

As their common name implies, Sage Grouse are birds of the great sagebrush deserts of the West. They were first reported by Lewis and Clark on their expedition, and were painted by John James Audubon from study skins obtained by the two explorers.

Although almost every Western pioneer and rancher ate the sagey flesh of these large grouse, very little was known of their mating behavior until their strutting grounds were carefully studied in the early 1940s. Since then, they have become one of the most intensively studied of the arena species and many thousands of spectators have watched their early-dawn strutting spectaculars.

In late winter, those Sage Grouse that escaped the shots of hunters and attacks of predators, band together in large flocks of both sexes in which the males feed side by side in peace and harmony. Then, in late March, the males leave the wintering flocks and begin to converge on the ancestral mating areas known as strutting grounds. These open areas in the sagebrush often measure 200 yards (180 meters) wide by a half-mile (1,609 meters) long. They are used year after year by the same population of grouse. In one instance, the grouse returned even after a road was built that completely bisected their strutting ground.

Unlike the Uganda kob, an arena antelope which allows only the most dominant males a place on the stamping ground, each cock in a Sage Grouse population will have its own court, a rectangular area of the main strutting ground about eight by twelve feet (2.4 by 4 meters) in size. Only the four or five courts near the very center of the ground have any social or sexual status, and every cock competes with his rivals for one of these bits of real estate.

No hens are in the area when the cocks first arrive on the strutting ground. All of their displaying is done to intimidate their competitors — and what a magnificent display these seven-pound (3.2-kilogram) roosters put on.

With long tails spread fanwise like a strutting turkey gobbler and wings dropping almost to the ground, heads are thrown back to reveal a beautiful contrast of black throat bordered by pure white breast. A pair of bright orange, unfeathered air sacks, normally hidden by the breast feathers, expand like small balloons as they are puffed-up to near the bursting point. While thus displaying, the cocks produce low, staccato grunts, intermingled with sounds like the purring of a huge cat.

In this manner they jockey for position, the more dominant males intimidating their inferiors until the elite of the population occupies the four or five master courts on which almost all mating will take place.

When the hens arrive, they congregate in the courts of the master cocks — all other males in the population are ignored. The master cocks, however, are not the only males on the court, for each is closely watched by his nearest rival, a subdominant cock, who waits patiently to take his place should the master drop from sheer exhaustion — which he often does. In addition, two or three guard cocks attend the court of each master cock. Their function appears to be one of keeping order in what could be utter chaos.

Field studies reveal that about 75 percent of the mating in a Sage Grouse population is done by the four or five master cocks, and most of the balance of the subdominate males who wait their turns. A very few matings involve the eight to fifteen guard cocks.

After a female has mated, she goes off by herself into the sagebrush to

114

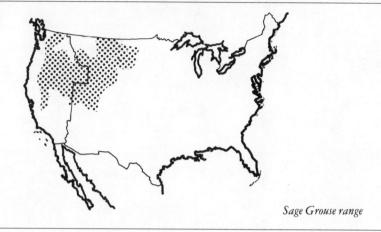

Sage Grouse range

lay her clutch of eight to fifteen greenish-white to olive-buff eggs. She alone incubates them for about 22 days, until the precocial (active early) chicks hatch. Like young domestic chickens, they are running about as soon as their down is dry and begin immediately to pick up food the mother scratches out for them.

During most of the summer, hens and chicks feed together on the flats, while males range in bachelor groups on the higher ridges. In late August or early September, the cocks come down to join the hens and juveniles for the fall and winter season, and large flocks are again the rule.

The winter fare of Sage Grouse is composed almost entirely of the leaves of sagebrush. Many other plants and some insects are consumed during other times of the year. Sagebrush is absolutely necessary as habitat for these great birds, and they disappear completely in areas where it is removed to provide more grass for domestic livestock.

The manner in which arena behavior evolved is one of the great mysteries of animal life. It is found in such distantly related life forms as antelope, wasps, and grouse, but is very similar in each case.

A strange fact discovered in studying arena behavior is that females are attracted to the property, not to the male that owns it. When a master cock is displaced by a subdominant rival, the females visit the new owner of the master court, even though he was completely ignored when he was the proprietor of an adjacent but less desirable piece of real estate.

*When facing danger a scorpion raises its potent tail
high over its back.*

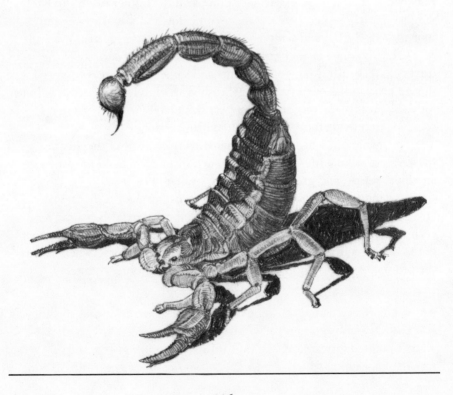

26

N ature's Living Hypodermic:
The evolution of stinging devices oc-
curred independently in many groups of animals. These biotic (living)
hypodermic needles have two purposes: To stun or kill other animals for
food or to discourage predators from making a meal of the stinging critter.

In the West, one of the most famous stinging animals is a strange
relative of spiders called a scorpion. Although we usually think of scorpions
as desert animals, they actually live in a wide range of habitats, from
tropical rainforest to temperate mountains.

With their crab-like pedalpalps, scorpions look as though they might
be crustaceans — related to crayfish and lobsters. However, these pinchers,
used for the same purpose by both groups of animals, are just a good
example of parallel evolution and are not indicative of a close relationship.

The abdominal region of a scorpion is divided into 12 segments. The
forward seven are wide and flat, while the rear five form a prehensile tail
that is usually carried curled over the animal's back.

The tip of the last abdominal segment is the real business end of a
scorpion. A curved and very sharp stinger with two tiny openings is
located there. Each opening is connected to one of two large venom glands
in the bulb-like swelling at the base of the stinger.

When facing danger or a potential meal, a scorpion spreads its pinchers
like an angry crab and raises its potent tail high over its back, with the
stinger pointed forward. When capturing and killing insects and other
small animals upon which it feeds, a scorpion grasps them firmly in both

pairs of pinchers and quickly drives home its venomous stinger.

Nocturnal habits make scorpions seem less common than they actually are. They spend the day hidden away under the loose bark of fallen logs or in similar cool and well-hidden nooks and crannies. Their soft bodies are relished by birds and they wouldn't last long if they were abroad during daylight hours. The tiny Elf Owl of the Sonoran desert captures scorpions at night and bites off their stingers before swallowing them whole.

Scorpions seem to be able to stand almost unbelievable heat for a short time. On several occasions I have thrown a log on a camp fire and then watched in awe as a scorpion that had hidden under the bark dashed across the hot embers in a futile attempt to escape the searing heat.

It's good sense when camped in scorpion country, to shake out boots and other clothing before putting them on in the morning. These pesky rascals have a nasty habit of choosing articles of apparel to hide in at the end of their night's wandering.

I learned this lesson the hard way years ago while sleeping out on the ground in the Texas desert. When I pulled on my pants, which had been laying under the foot of my sleeping bag, I felt a sharp pain in my left knee. In near panic, I slapped at my knee and then broke all records for removing a pair of jeans both legs at once. Inspection revealed one badly smashed scorpion and a tiny red spot on a knee that rapidly began to throb and soon swelled to twice normal size.

I was lucky — the scorpion was not one of the deadly varieties found in our Southwestern deserts. The United States has about 40 of the World's 650 species of scorpions, and their stings range from harmless to painful to deadly. The two species usually responsible for human deaths are *Centruroides sculpturatus* and *Centruroides gertschi*. Arizona alone recorded 64 human deaths to these two species in one 20-year period. In North America, including Mexico, more people are killed by scorpions than by venomous snakes.

The venom of scorpions is a neurotoxin (nerve poison) and kills by causing paralysis of the respiratory and cardiac muscles. Most victims are children and elderly people — few healthy adults suffer fatal stings.

Despite their fierce appearance and painful stings, scorpions are fascinating creatures that have a strange and interesting reproductive behavior. During a claw-to-claw nuptial dance — filmed and set to square-dance music in an old Walt Disney nature movie — the male deposits a sperm container on the ground. He then maneuvers his mate over this spermatophore so that it enters her genital orifice.

The gestation period for scorpions is from several months to as much as a year. The developing embryos are fed by tubes connected to the female's digestive system, a method remarkably similar to that of placental mammals.

Instead of hatching from eggs, young scorpions are born as fully formed replicas of their parents. They ride about on the mother's back for a week or two before striking out on their own. Scorpions mature in about a year.

27

P hantoms of the Prairie: When
Europeans first arrived in North America,
they found many animals that resembled Old World species. These often
were given the same names as their Eastern Hemisphere look-alikes, even
though they were not closely related.

The "antelopes" of Western North America are a good example. They
are similar to the true antelopes of Africa and Asia in being herd animals of
open country that are extremely fleet of foot. However, our antelopes
(which are correctly called Pronghorns) belong to a monotypic (single
living species) family found only in North America.

Pronghorns, *Antilocapra americana*, are in the family Antilocapridae,
with characteristics midway between those of deer in the family Cervidae
and those of sheep, goats, cattle, and true antelopes in the family Bovidae.
Cervids have branched antlers that are shed annually, while bovids sport
unbranched horns that are retained for their entire lives. Pronghorns have
horns with a single tiny branch or prong off the main beam. They shed the
outer covering each year but retain the inner bony core.

The Antilocapridae is an ancient family that roamed the West for
several millions of years, and our Pronghorn is the sole survivor. The bones
of its ancient relatives — one had four horns — have been found in many
archaeological digs. Why the other species died off is not known, but they
probably just failed to adapt to a rapidly changing environment.

Deer-sized Pronghorns are the fastest running animals in the Western
Hemisphere. They can maintain a steady 40 miles (65 kilometers) per

hour for two to three miles (3 to 5 kilometers) and, when pressed, can exceed 60 miles (100 kilometers) per hour for short distances. They easily outran the now-extinct Prairie Wolves that were their major predators. Only by running in relays were wolves able to dine on a healthy Pronghorn.

Although beautifully marked, Pronghorns blend in surprisingly well with the drab colors of the sagebrush country they inhabit. Their coat varies from pale-buff to bright-cinnamon, with white undersides, rump, and twin neck stripes. Their hooves, muzzle, mane, ear tips, and horns are black, to lend a striking accent. The long white hairs on their rumps can be rapidly elevated to flash signals like a heliograph.

Pronghorns' eyes, as large as those of a horse, are believed to be the equivalent of a human's aided by eight-power binoculars. They are extremely alert to any strange objects in the open prairie, and instantly flash a danger signal which other pronghorns can see two miles (3 kilometers) away. Once they start running, they seldom stop until they have put several miles between themselves and the potential danger.

Prior to the uncontrolled slaughter of wildlife during the last century, an estimated 50- to 100-million Pronghorns roamed the prairies of the West. When the shooting orgy was finally snuffed out by the enactment and enforcement of game laws, only a few thousand remained. Under protection, these have now increased to several hundred thousand.

Pronghorns once were common in California's Central Valleys, but the last reported sighting was in Fresno County in 1954. Small herds still roam the sparsely populated counties of Lassen and Modoc and offer Californians the only chance to view these prairie phantoms under wild and free conditions.

One secret in finding Pronghorns is to look for white spots in the sagebrush. Their white rumps are their most conspicuous coloration and usually are seen long before the outline of the animal is discerned. They are very curious about strange objects they can't identify, and sometimes a concealed observer can coax one into camera range by waving a white rag on a stick.

With their sharp eyesight and open country living, Pronghorns are difficult to approach within rifle range. Although the practice is illegal, many are killed by chasing and shooting them from offroad vehicles. Unfortunately, game laws are difficult to enforce in the Western states where one warden may patrol hundreds of square miles.

Although a significant amount of legal and illegal shooting of Pronghorns occurs, the greatest threats are loss of their sagebrush habitat

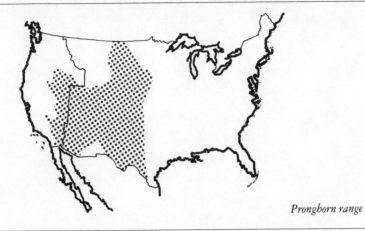

Pronghorn range

and the building of sheep-tight fences. Millions of acres of sagebrush are being cleared by spraying with herbicides to increase grass for cattle and sheep on public lands in the West. Pronghorns are browsers, not grazers, and when the brush is cleared they and the Sage Grouse disappear.

Pronghorns refuse to jump fences, but easily crawl between strands of barbed wire. However, when woven sheep fences are erected, their movements are disrupted. These fences, which are sometimes illegally installed on public lands by sheepmen, become a death trap when Pronghorns, driven by a howling blizzard, pile up at fence corners and freeze to death.

Pocket Gophers feel ill at ease in sunshine and blue sky.

28

Pocket Gophers Till the Soil: If you ever have watched in disbelief as a plant grew shorter and finally disappeared right before your eyes, you may not have been imagining things. You may have witnessed the food-gathering activity of a strange little burrowing rodent, the Pocket Gopher.

Like the insect-eating moles to which they are distantly related, Pocket Gophers have evolved as underground animals. Their wide distribution and large numbers testify to their success at this life style. They occur throughout Western North America, from central Canada to Mexico. They are found in almost any habitat with soil conditions suitable for digging their elaborate systems of tunnels.

So completely have Pocket Gophers adapted to their fossorial (digging) existence that they seldom surface except to bring up a load of excavated soil. Even then, they seem to feel ill-at-ease in the world of sunshine and blue sky. They seldom show more than head and shoulders at the burrow entrance as they push out a pile of dirt and quickly back down into the security of their dark passageways.

Pocket Gophers are rat-sized rodents with tiny ears and small, beady eyes. Their almost naked tails are short, and their front feet have long, curved claws adapted for digging. Their common name comes from fur-lined, reversible cheek pouches, which open onto either side of the head and can be stuffed full of food, even with the mouth closed.

Although they differ in many other ways, the most obvious difference between Pocket Gophers and moles is their dentition (arrangement of teeth). Moles have long rows of slender, pointed teeth well adapted to preying on insects. Gophers, like all other rodents, have two pairs of long, curved, chisel-like incisors that are perfect instruments for eating plant roots and stems.

A mole's teeth are rather inconspicuous when the animal's mouth is closed, but, open or closed, the Pocket Gopher can't hide its outsized choppers. They are arranged so the lips close behind them, enabling the gopher to gnaw through a stubborn chunk of hard-packed earth without getting a mouth full of dirt.

In typical rodent fashion, the curved incisors of a gopher continue to grow during the entire life of the animal. If not worn down by continual use, they grow in a complete circle and pierce its head. This can happen when a tooth is broken off and its opposite in the other jaw has no surface to wear against.

The most obvious evidence of the presence of gophers is the small mounds of dirt left on the surface. They usually are fan-shaped, with the burrow entrance to one side. Those of moles are symmetrical, like miniature volcanoes.

A tunnel system may be many yards long, the work of a single animal. Gophers are solitary and highly territorial, and vicious fights erupt when a trespasser invades the territory. Only during courtship will a male leave his own tunnel and seek a mate on her home ground. After mating, the male goes his own way and the female remains to raise the litter of kits in her burrow.

During this springtime courtship period the males often incautiously wander about above ground in broad daylight. It is then they may literally lose their head over a female as they fall victim to a soaring Red-tailed Hawk or other predator.

Gophers are less prolific than most rodents, giving birth to only a single litter of four or five each year. A newborn gopher is anything but beautiful. It is pink and naked, with a skin three sizes too big. It weighs about one-fifth of an ounce (six grams). Its eyes and ears are sealed tightly shut. The eyes won't open until shortly before it leaves its mother's burrow at six to eight weeks of age.

High-country hikers often are puzzled by strange cylinders of packed soil they find on the ground after the winter snow has melted away. These are castings made when gophers, which are active all winter, cram soil into tunnels made in the snow. After the snow melts, the soil plugs remain as perfect tracings of snow caves used to dispose of surplus soil.

In the alpine tundra of the Sierra Nevada and the Rockies, Pocket

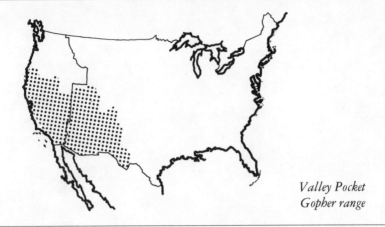

*Valley Pocket
Gopher range*

Gophers are responsible for beautiful plant communities called gopher gardens. Their burrowing and feeding activities disrupt the thick, sedgy carpets of tundra vegetation and allow an invasion of colorful wildflowers such as lupine, larkspur, columbine and skypilot. These natural gardens are alive with brightly colored butterflies and gem-like hummingbirds. They perform the vital plant reproductive task of transporting pollen in exchange for sweet nectar from the glands of each blossom.

The dense tundra may be even further disturbed by predators, such as Badgers and Coyotes, digging out gophers. This soil upheaval results in the increased moisture needed by shallower-rooted flowers. In time, a gopher garden again may be taken over by tundra, with its cushion-like, long-lived perennials, but this slow process takes many years to complete. In the meantime, these industrious little diggers will be establishing other gardens nearby in a form of natural crop rotation.

The turning over of soil is an important function of gophers and other burrowing animals. Nutrients tend to be leached downward in the soil, and eventually get too deep for shallow-rooted plants. When gophers, moles, and earthworms deposit their soil piles on the surface, they bring these all-important plant foods back into circulation and loosen the soil to allow better penetration of water and oxygen.

Although considered unwelcome guests in a well-tended garden, Pocket Gophers are essential members of natural communities to which they belong. They act as tillers of the soil and are important links in the complex food webs that hold together the living fabric of the ecosystem.

Voles are close relatives of Arctic Lemmings.

29

A Vole's Life is Brief But Busy: Voles, also called meadow mice, seldom are seen but their neatly clipped runways can be found in grassy areas throughout the West. Close examination of almost any uncultivated grassy field or mountain meadow will reveal an elaborate maze of narrow passageways used by these prolific little rodents to travel about in search of their favorite plant foods.

The term vole is really a catchall, used to designate any one of many closely related and similar-appearing rodents that are almost impossible to tell apart in the field. Many can be positively identified only by a close examination of certain characteristics of teeth and skulls. In general appearance, they are fat, medium-sized mice, with small ears almost hidden in their soft fur. Their tails are short and well covered with hair, and their eyes are like tiny black beads.

One of the most notable characteristics of voles is their almost unbelievable reproductive rate. Females mate for the first time when just over three weeks of age and may give birth to as many as 17 litters of from five to ten young each during the first year of their lives — if they are fortunate enough to live that long. Most voles die of old age before their first birthday, if predators, disease, or parasites don't cut their life span even shorter.

Voles are close relatives of the lemmings of the Arctic tundra, made famous by their periodic suicidal migrations into the sea. (These mass movements occur at roughly four-year intervals, when populations peak at numbers far in excess of the capacity of the habitat. Lemmings probably don't intentionally commit suicide, but simply see the ocean as just another stream or pond to be crossed in their frenzied search for uncrowded territory.)

Like lemmings, voles also experience cyclic population explosions in which their numbers reach incredible highs, but they don't relieve the pressure by migration. In an ideal habitat, the normal vole population may be about 50 individuals per acre. During a population explosion in the Humboldt Valley of Nevada in 1907, they reached the fantastic density of 8,000 to 12,000 per acre.

Population densities of this magnitude can't last long, but while they do the habitat may be severely damaged as every bit of edible plant material is consumed. Fortunately, the predator population also increases as hawks, owls, Coyotes, Bobcats, foxes, snakes, and other meat-eaters move in to take advantage of the easy feeding. These natural checks are more effective than the poisons used by humans, but many valuable predators die as a result of eating rodents already dying from poisoned grain.

A population eruption of the California Vole, *Microtus californicus*, occured in the Sacramento Valley in the late 1960s. I remember watching small flocks of Barn Owls, normally solitary nocturnal hunters, gorging on voles in broad daylight. The voles were feeding on the blossoms of star thistle, and the owls were plucking dinner off the tops of thistle like ripe fruit out of a tree.

Although a female vole sneaks away from her newborn litter within a few hours to mate and become pregnant again, she is a doting mother who will clack her teeth in the face of an advancing Gopher Snake or weasel to protect her family. Her nursery is a beautifully woven, hollow, globe-like nest of grass, luxuriantly lined with soft plant fibers such as milkweed floss or cattail down.

Newborn voles are tiny, blind, deaf, and hairless creatures, whose internal organs can be seen through their delicate pink skin. They grow rapidly, and by the age of four days are well covered with fuzzy fur, and have cut their sharp incisors by the sixth or seventh. In another day or two their eyes and ears also become functional.

By the time a baby vole reaches two weeks of age, it is two inches (5 centimeters) long and foraging for its own food. If it is a female, it will be pregnant with its first litter in just another week or so, although it won't complete its own growth until three months of age.

The males reach sexual maturity about a week later than the females.

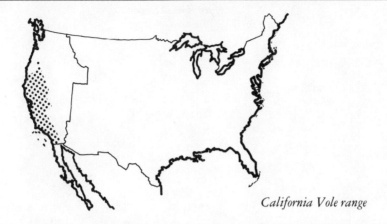

California Vole range

Thus, they will have to wander off to seek first mates among females in adjacent territories. This helps assure that genetic traits are well shuffled among the population so that undesirable mutations are not perpetuated by inbreeding.

Although voles' runways are the most evident signs of their presence, they also build a system of underground tunnels to flee predators and seek shelter from the elements. Voles don't hibernate and those that live where winters are white use snow tunnels to reach their food supply.

I have been amused for hours watching agile Coyotes digging voles out of the snow in mountain meadows and have marveled at their success. They seem to locate their prey by using both their sensitive ears and nose. A little yodel-dog will remain frozen in place for minutes at a time, with nose pressed against the snow and ears cocked to pick up the tiniest sound from below. Suddenly, in a motion almost too quick to follow, it will dig rapidly with its front paws and plunge its delicate pointed muzzle into the snow. Seldom will it fail to come up with a fat meadow mouse.

30

The Ring-necked Pheasant, One of Man's Successful Transplants: In almost all cases, relocation of plants or animals to places they were never found naturally has proven to be at least a serious mistake. Sometimes, such as Starlings in North America and rabbits in Australia, intentional redistributions have been ecological disasters of the first magnitude.

It is refreshing then, to point out one introduction that is an almost unqualified success. This is the Ring-necked Pheasant, *Phasianus colchicus*, a colorful game bird that has become such a familiar sight in agricultural lands that many Americans think it is a true native.

Ring-necks are native to Asia, but were introduced to Europe during the days of the Roman Empire. Pheasant hunting with long bow or crossbow became a popular sport in England long before the advent of the shotgun.

It was a longing by transplanted Englishmen for pheasant hunting as they had known it at home that resulted in the first attempts at stocking this species in the New World. As early as 1730, a dozen pairs were released in New York and these were followed by an untold number of others throughout the New England colonies.

These early introductions of birds from Europe had one thing in common — they all resulted in failure. Predators, poachers, and the elements each took its toll, and few were ever seen alive after being released.

It wasn't until a century and a half later that Ring-necked Pheasants finally became established in the New World. The first successful plant differed from the earlier failures in one important way — the birds released were native stock from China, not the descendants of pen-raised birds from Europe.

The two shipments of Chinese pheasants were paid for by Judge Owen N. Denny, the U.S. consul in Shanghai, from his own funds. The first lot of 60 were released near Denny's home in the vicinity of Portland, Oregon, in 1881, but all apparently perished. A second shipment of 28 took, and in a single decade had become so numerous that the state of Oregon declared an open season to hunt them. An estimated 50,000 were killed during that first legal pheasant hunt in America in 1891.

Oregon's established flock served as a nucleus for introductions attempted in all of the other 47 states. California jumped on the pheasant bandwagon in 1889, with a release of 140 birds, and by 1909 was in the game-farm business to raise birds for release.

In the early days of pheasant propagation, many birds were wasted by releasing them into unsuitable habitat. Fertile valleys with agriculture devoted mainly to grain crops were favored, and Sacramento Valley's rice fields were a natural. Nearly half of the hundreds of thousands of pheasants killed in California each year are taken in the Sacramento Valley.

A number of Ring-neck attributes combine to make it a top success as an introduced game species. First, unlike its relative, the domestic chicken, the pheasant can be raised in captivity without becoming tame. Pen-raised birds become just as wary as wild-raised ones as soon as they are given their freedom.

Secondly, male Ring-necks are polygamous — they mate with a number of different hens and are in no way involved in raising the chicks. This means that a certain percentage of the roosters can be shot each season without affecting the reproductive capacity of the population. In addition, rooster-only hunting is made practical because of the great dissimilarity of the sexes — males are larger, much more brightly colored, and have longer tails than females. They also help hunters identify them by cackling loudly when flushed.

A major reason for the pheasants ability to quickly populate suitable habitat is its fecundity. The hens lay from 6 to 14 olive-buff eggs in a neat ground nest usually well hidden in grass or other low cover. Large clutches of two dozen or more eggs that are sometimes found are the work of two or more hens laying in the same nest.

Pheasant hens remain on the nest when danger approaches and depend upon their cryptic (concealing) coloring to conceal them and their eggs.

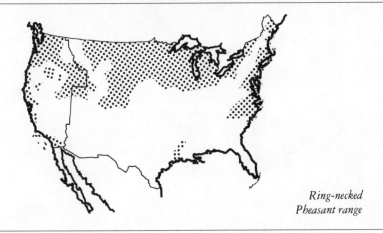

*Ring-necked
Pheasant range*

This habit of close setting results in many being killed by mowing machines and other farm equipment. Flushing bars mounted ahead of the machine successfully reduce this type of loss.

Pheasant chicks are precocial (early active) and leave the nest as soon as they hatch and their ample down has dried. They follow the hen about in search of food, rather than waiting helplessly to be fed like altricial nestlings (those that are helpless for a long period of time). They are far less vulnerable to predators than young birds left alone in the nest while the parents forage. They grow wing feathers and can fly when still very small, another factor that contributes to their survival.

Ring-neck hens are fearless in protecting their broods and will rout predators larger than themselves. While on a field trip to Gray Lodge Wildlife Area, my students and I watched two pheasant hens drive off a feral (turned wild) house cat that had quite likely threatened their chicks which were hidden in the grass along the road shoulder. The cat was in full retreat and was closely followed by the two angry mothers, who hit it repeatedly as they ran and flew in hot pursuit. The cat was knocked off its feet several times before it managed to escape.

Bushy-tailed Woodrats live in jumbled boulder fields.

31

N ative Rats of The West: Not all rats are filthy, gaunt, scaly-tailed rodents that attack sleeping ghetto children and despoil human food supplies. Our native woodrats, genus *Neotoma*, are clean, furry-tailed creatures, that frequent wild lands throughout the West and seldom cause problems for human-kind.

Woodrats resemble their noxious, introduced cousins in general form, but can be distinguished by several easily observed characteristics. All woodrats have well-furred tails, and the Bushy-tailed Woodrat, *Neotoma cinerea*, the mountaineer of the clan, has a tail like a squirrel. The tails of introduced rats have just a few coarse hairs that do little to hide the scaly skin beneath. The underparts of our native rats are a pleasing white, those of the Old World immigrants are a dirty gray.

Woodrats may take up residence in abandoned cabins or ranch buildings, but usually choose natural sites for their stick nests.

The Desert Woodrat, *Neotoma lepida*, constructs its nest on the ground near the base of various cacti or desert shrubs. The nest usually is small, with tunnels and living quarters dug in the soil below. The nest and surrounding area are liberally covered with the fierce, spiny pads of cholla cactus, making a fortress virtually unapproachable by four-footed predators. How the rats are able to transport the several bushels of these spiny pads without being impaled is a mystery. Desert hikers soon learn how difficult it is to extract the barbed spines of cholla.

The Dusky-footed Woodrat, *Neotoma fuscipes*, which is found in the foothill chaparral and oak woodland habitats, builds an immense stick nest that may reach eight feet (2.4 meters) in diameter and six feet (1.8 meters) in height. Although the larger nests represent the life's work of a series of owners, they never are occupied by more than one adult at a time.

When a woodrat falls victim to predation, disease, or old age, its home is promptly taken over by another, who adds material to that already present. There is some evidence that an old or debilitated animal may be driven from a home by a younger or stronger rival and forced to live in less desirable quarters, but it is usually death, not eviction, that changes ownership.

The nests of Dusky-footed Woodrats are usually placed at the base of a multitrunked chaparral shrub or low-branched live oak. They are stout nests, of large twigs and branches well interwoven, and are almost impregnable to larger predators.

The Bushy-tailed Woodrats of the higher mountains and desert canyons build smaller stick nests in caves, rock crevices, and boulder fields. Many of the cave sites have been occupied for thousands of years by untold generations of woodrats — their urine, feces, and food wastes cover the floor in thick, tar-like deposits. Preserved in this material will be seeds, pollen, and other recognizable plant material gathered by past generations.

Scientists have used these rat middens (refuse heaps) to study the past plant life and climatic history of the areas where they are found. These remains provide a chronological record of the past with the oldest material on the bottom and most recent on top.

Rat middens have revealed that many desert regions once were covered with coniferous forests, evidence that the climate then was much wetter than it is now.

One unusual habit of woodrats has given them their alternate common names — pack rats or trade rats. They regularly carry small objects back to their nests. If they encounter something more attractive while en route, they often drop what they are carrying and pick up the new treasure.

This trading routine didn't go over too well with early miners or cowboys, who would wake up to find a shiny pebble or empty brass cartridge case where a watch or dentures had been placed the night before. No one will every know how many partnerships were terminated or friendships destroyed by such trade-rat dirty tricks.

A woodrat's nest holds more than just ornaments collected by a series of owners. These huge stick piles are wildlife hotels for a fantastic array of life forms. Lizards, snakes, salamanders, rabbits, mice, shrews, spiders, ticks, and many types of insects have been counted among the uninvited

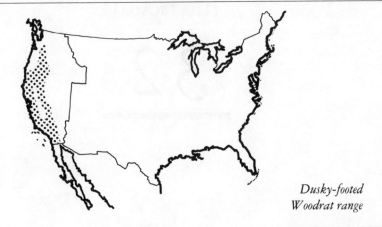

*Dusky-footed
Woodrat range*

guests. The woodrat, however, cares little about most of these freeloaders. Except for the larger snakes who may repay hospitality by dining on their host.

Each woodrat nest is the center of a well-worn system of pathways used by the rodents on their nightly excursions to gather food. They eat some plant food where they find it and carry some back to the nests to store for later use. These stored provisions are usually seeds, nuts, or berries that will keep well. Woodrats don't hibernate. They depend upon their storehouses for winter survival.

The natural food habits of woodrats have resulted in little conflict with humans — they have thus escaped the extermination campaigns directed against many of their rodent relatives. They themselves are important food items for a list that reads like the Who's Who of Western Predatordom. They are hunted by Coyotes, foxes, Bobcats, Badgers, skunks, bears, owls, snakes, and many others. They escape predation by hawks because of their nocturnal habits.

The Bushy-tailed Woodrats that reside in the jumbled boulder fields of the Sierra make up much of the summer diet of the rare and beautiful Pine Martens and their tiny but fierce cousins, the Longtail Weasels. In the rocky canyon lands of the arid Southwest, the graceful Ringtails hunt woodrats in their cliff-face homes in vertical exposures that would give a rock climber a case of vertigo.

32

C icadas Signal Summer: Just as
the cheery songs of birds signal the arrival
of spring, the monotonous buzz of cicadas portends the arrival of Western
summer. Cicadas are large insects, known to many as locusts or harvest
flies. They have a remarkable natural history. Some 1,500 species are
known to science and 200 of these are found in North America.

Although cicadas are the giants of the Homopteran insect order, their
close relatives include such tiny forms as aphids, leafhoppers, froghoppers,
and scale insects. Cicadas vary in size from ½-inch (13 millimeters) long to
an Australian species more than two inches (51 millimeters) with a
five-inch wingspread.

Cicadas are famous for long childhoods and extremely brief lives as
adults. The juveniles, called nymphs, spend as much as 17 years in almost
endless tunneling deep in the soil before emerging to become adults.
Then, after a few days of mating and egg-laying, they undergo a rapid and
pre-programmed death.

Future generations of cicadas are contained in tiny eggs inserted into
the bark of twigs on trees and shrubs by the female's sharp spear-like
ovipositor (egg depositing organ). The only economic damage done by
these insects is this mechanical piercing of the bark, but it can affect the
health of a plant if enough cicadas use it for a brood chamber.

The eggs hatch in about a week into tiny nymphs that quickly drop to
the ground and burrow into the soil. There they live on energy they tap
from the roots of trees and shrubs with their piercing-sucking mouthparts.

Cicadas have a built-in calendar.

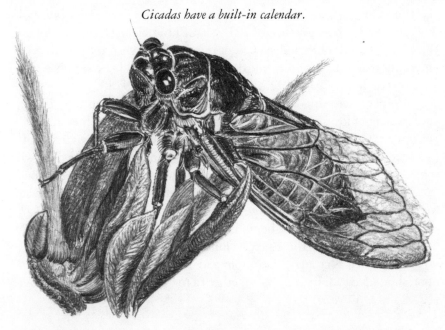

Cicada nymphs are equipped with powerful fossorial (burrowing) forelegs, which allow them to move easily through even hard-packed soil.

After a period of from 2 to 17 years, depending on species, the nymphs dig toward the surface and leave the soil for the last time. They climb into a shrub or low tree and attach themselves firmly with their strong claws. Soon their nymphal skins split down the back and the adults emerge.

One of the astounding mysteries of cicada biology is the precise timing of their emergence. The so-called Periodical Cicadas (also known as 17-Year Locusts) emerge every 13 or 17 years under the control of some remarkable timing device that tells the burrowing juvenile insects it is time to return to the world of blue sky and sunshine. No one knows what triggers the emergence, but it seems unlikely the nymphs are able to communicate with each other through several feet of soil.

A cicada emergence usually takes place at night, giving the new adults a chance to fully expand their wings before becoming vulnerable to efficient daytime predators, such as insectivorous birds. After a major emergence, the vegetation is often covered by the shed nymphal skins.

The broods of the Periodical Cicadas overlap, so that an emergence is taking place somewhere nearly every summer. In the West, cicadas have two- to five-year cycles and are known as Dogday Cicadas, because many emerge during the so-called dogdays of July. The Periodical Cicadas, which are found in the Eastern United States, appear in May or June.

Broods of 13- and 17-year cicadas may occur in the same area but will emerge together only once every 221 years. Entomologists have catalogued the various broods of Periodical Cicadas since 1893, when the brood emerging that year was given the designation of Brood I. Brood I has appeared in 1893, 1910, 1927, 1944, 1961, and in 1978.

Another interesting attribute is their sound-producing ability. The endless song of lovesick males is a characteristic sound of summer in the Southwest. Only the males sing, but both males and females have special ears that detect these mating sounds. Each of the many species has its own song and, as with the birds, one can learn to identify them by sound alone.

The song of the male cicada is apparently a mechanism to get the sexes together for that brief interchange of genetic material that will begin another cycle. Science is just beginning to unravel some of the mysteries of biological calendars — those precise innate timing devices that allow organisms, such as cicadas, to complete marvelous life-cycles which depend upon short-lived adults coming together to mate on just one right day out of as many as 17 years.

33

T rickery in the Mating Game:
Despite a rather ominous common name,
scorpionflies are innocuous animals that neither bite nor sting. What's
more, these little-known and very primitive insects eat absolutely nothing
of any real economic importance to humans and seldom are even seen near
human abodes.

Entomologists have classified scorpionflies in the tiny insect order
Mecoptera, that numbers only 400 species in the world with about 75 in
North America. In contrast, the very successful beetles, in order
Coleoptera, have more than 290,000 known species worldwide and at least
28,000 are on this continent.

The name scorpionfly comes from the strange bulbous-shaped genitalia
(reproductive organs) of the males of some species. They are carried curved
forward over their backs much like the business end of a real scorpion. The
true scorpions, of course, are not insects at all, but arachnids, a group that
also includes such animals as spiders, ticks, and mites.

All scorpionflies have strange, elongated snouts with chewing-type
mouthparts at the very tip. These effective mandibles allow their
predaceous owners to chew up the bodies of other insects. Not all
scorpionflies are predators, however. Some are simply scavengers that feed
on dead and dying insects, and others are omnivores that include some
plant material in their diets.

Except for a few species which are entirely wingless, scorpionflies have
two pairs of membraneous wings almost identical in size and shape. Their

Scorpionflies are neither scorpions nor flies.

legs are long and slender, a characteristic that often results in their being mistaken for crane flies (like all true flies, crane flies have only a single pair of wings).

Scorpionflies have long thread-like antennae reaching, in some species, almost half the length of the entire body. These organs contain sensitive nerve endings providing their owners with a tactile means of perceiving the world around them.

Despite the small numbers of this order, scorpionflies are of great interest to entomologists for they provide an important connecting link in insect evolution. They first appear in the fossil record for the Permian period of more than 200 million years ago, and are thought to be ancestral to such later forms as butterflies, moths, true flies, and caddisflies.

Even though they were the prototypes for many highly successful modern insects, scorpionflies themselves appear to be a dying breed. During the period of their dominance in the Permian, they constituted about 9 percent of the total number of insect species. By the Mesozoic, this had fallen to 3.7 percent and to 0.16 percent by the Tertiary. Now, in modern times, they constitute only an infinitesimal 0.035 percent of the known number of insect forms.

One of the most common members of the scorpionfly order found in the West is the Hangingfly, *Bittacus chlorostigma*. This relatively large predatory species is about one inch (2.5 centimeters) in length and has a single bright yellow spot in each of its four clear membraneous wings.

Hangingflies have developed an unusual way of capturing prey. They hang from a perch by their front legs and capture other insects by snatching them with their highly developed hind pair.

Hangingflies are very common in high grass in the shade of oaks and other deciduous trees in late spring and early summer. It was in such a setting that I was able to observe and photograph a strange mating behavior I find no mention of in the rather sparse literature on this species.

On this occasion, I watched several male Hangingflies capture a softbodied insect larva and apparently offer it to a nearby female. Mating took place while the female fed upon the food morsel clutched in the rear talons of the male as both hung from a blade of grass by their forelegs.

After mating, the males would take back their gifts and fly off in search of another hungry female. I watched one male entice three different females with the same moth larva before most of it was consumed. Female Hangingflies are known to resort to cannibalism and this may be a way for the male to assure he does not become a meal during the mating game.

The offering of food to entice females has been well documented in the dance flies. These very tiny predators are true flies that are often observed in dense mating swarms hovering almost like a smoke cloud in the sunshine.

Like scorpionflies, male dance flies capture other insects as an offering to the females in the swarm. However, the dance fly males have modified this technique to what must be one of the ultimate acts of male chauvinism.

The males of some species wrap the food offering in a frothy web which keeps the female occupied for some time attempting to unwrap her wedding present. The males of other species carry the game to the ultimate limit — they simply wrap up some inedible object and present it to an unsuspecting female. By the time she has gotten through the many layers of gift wrapping and discovers she has been tricked, mating is over and the male is off searching for another victim.

Many old-timers believed the Ringtail was a cross between a cat and a Raccoon.

146

34

A Graceful Climber: My nomination for the most graceful and aesthetically appealing of our Western mammals is the lovely little Ringtail, *Bassariscus astutus*. It is a small relative of the Raccoon, and is only slightly larger than a Gray Squirrel. It has no close competitors in beauty or climbing ability.

The Ringtail has many common names — wood cat, miner's cat, coon cat, ringtailed cat, squirrel cat, and American civet cat are just a few. Its generic name, *Bassariscus*, comes from a Greek word meaning little fox. Many, but not all, taxonomists (classifiers) place the Ringtail in the family Procyonidae, which includes such diverse members as the Raccoon, Giant Panda, and Coati.

Two species of Ringtail are known to science, only one of which is found in the United States. It ranges from Southern Mexico to Oregon and can be found wherever suitable habitat is available. Its favorite haunts are steep-walled rocky canyons in arid foothills. The Ringtail lives mostly in the Upper Sonoran Life Zone — regions which have a climate similar to the higher elevations of the Sonoran desert of Arizona and Mexico. It also can be found in a few locations on the floor of the Central Valleys where dense vegetation remains along water courses such as the Sacramento River.

An adult Ringtail is about 30 inches (76 centimeters) long from the tip of its delicately pointed muzzle to the end of its bushy tail. Over half of this length is tail, which sports alternate bands of dark brown and white that give the animal its correct common name. A pair of large liquid black eyes, ringed by distinct white spectacles contrast with its golden-buff head and body, and its large triangular ears give it a fox-like appearance. Its tiny five-toed paws with semi-retractile claws are far more cat-like than those of its Raccoon cousins.

Many old-timers in the American Southwest believed the Ringtail was a cross between a cat and a Raccoon. These two animals, however, are too distantly related to ever produce a viable hybrid, even if they were to mate.

While Ringtails are relatively common in zoos and animal exhibits, few people ever see a wild one. This is not because they are extremely scarce, but because of their shy and night-roaming habits. Unlike many other nocturnal mammals which may begin their nightly wanderings in the early hours of dusk, Ringtails wait until absolute darkness has fallen over their canyon homes. They return to their den — in a hollow log, rock crevice, or abandoned shack — long before the first glow of dawn.

Like their Raccoon and Coati relatives, Ringtails are omnivorous — they feed on both plant and animal material. Small rodents, such as deer mice and woodrats, make up a large part of their meat diet, but they also eat many insects, as evidenced by remains in their droppings. Fruit is eaten when available — the berries of manzanita, cascara, and toyon are particular favorites.

Ringtails have few peers when it comes to agility. Even perpendicular cliff faces present no barrier to these tiny mountaineers. If a vertical crack is available, they may ascend by the technique known as chimney stemming — putting feet against one surface and back against the other and wedging their way upward. If a crack is too wide for this method, they simply go up or down by ricocheting from surface to surface, using their ample tail as a balancing organ.

A rear foot design also found in tree squirrels and some other climbing mammals allows the Ringtail to descend headfirst any sheer face that offers a few toe-holds. The hind feet can be pointed straight back along the body axis and rotated 180 degrees to allow the animal to hang by its hind toes.

A male Ringtail, unlike the promiscuous male Raccoon, is a devoted father who helps raise the yearly litter of up to four kittens. Field studies have shown that permanent pair bonds are formed and the male is separated from his mate only for a brief period while she is nursing the kittens. As soon as they are weaned, the male returns to the fold. He hunts to provide solid food and accompanies the family on nightly excursions on which the young learn to hunt and forage for themselves. At about four months of age, the kittens are on their own and seek their own territories.

Dr. Gene Trapp, mammalogist at California State University, Sacramento, earned his doctorate studying Ringtail behavior in Zion

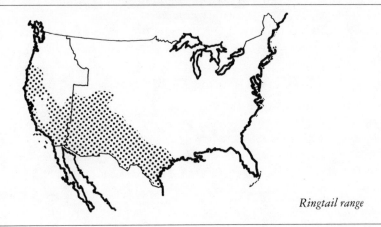

Ringtail range

National Park in Utah. One pair of Ringtails Trapp studied lived in the park but visited a feeding station maintained by a retired couple near the park entrance. The Ringtails, named Andy and Missy, returned to the feeding station for eight consecutive years, and even brought each new family with them to learn the art of obtaining free handouts of bananas and raisins. Andy and Missy stopped coming to the feeder in 1975. Trapp fears they either succumbed to old age or met with foul play.

Speed and agility make Ringtails relatively safe from most mammalian predators. A few are taken by Great Horned Owls, but their nocturnal habits protect them from the diurnal (daytime) birds of prey. Steel-jaw traps are the greatest hazard they face. Ringtails are not at all trap-shy and are easily caught even in cage-type live traps, a technique Trapp used in Zion to capture animals which he fitted with radio-collars.

Ringtail fur has little commercial value and trappers rarely trap specifically for them. However, because they are less wary than the usual target species, such as fox, Bobcat, and Coyote, many Ringtails die needlessly in sets placed for these heavily trapped animals. Ringtails are protected by law in California but this, unfortunately, does not protect them from traps. One trapper in Northern California wrote on his fur-trapper's report to Fish and Game that he caught 10 Ringtails but threw the pelts away because they were protected.

Several states, including Florida, have banned the use of steel-jaw traps for killing wildlife. There are humane laws that protect domestic animals from treatment far less brutal than is dealt out by these antiquated torture devices. Why do we permit wildlife to suffer? If the individual states fail to act, the federal government should outlaw these archaic contraptions that are a holdover from an age when little compassion was shown for the suffering of the so-called lower animals.

Desert Tortoises have changed very little in several million years.

35

T anks of the Desert: The Desert Tortoise, *Gopherus agassizi*, a distant relative of amphibious turtles, is marvelously adapted to live in the dry deserts of the West. It is found in California's desert regions as well as in southern Nevada, the very southwestern tip of Utah, western Arizona, and northwestern Mexico.

It is the only species of tortoise occurring naturally within California. It is a threatened reptile and the Desert Tortoise Preserve has been established near Lancaster, California, to protect it.

With a shell length of 12 inches (30 centimeters) in large adults, the Desert Tortoise is tiny when compared to its relatives, the giant tortoises of the Galapagos Islands. The carapace, or upper half of the shell, has a high-domed shape and is brown to gray in color. The plastron, or lower half, is yellowish and lacks the hinge found in the familiar box turtle of the East and Midwest.

The defense posture of the gentle Desert Tortoise involves withdrawing its head into its shell until only the tip of the nose can be seen and using heavily armored front and hind legs to plug the openings in the shell. In this position, none of its soft parts are exposed to predators' teeth or talons.

Desert Tortoises have been adapted to their arid habitat for several million years and have changed very little in that time. All members of their genus (group) are called gopher tortoises because they build long tunnels in the ground to escape the heat of summer days and for hibernation during the cold of winter.

As with all reptiles, Desert Tortoises are ectothermic, which means they have no internal mechanism for maintaining a constant body temperature. That makes them sensitive to heat and cold and they vary daily activity patterns to take advantage of the most favorable temperatures to be out and about. In the pleasant days of spring and fall, they are active at any time of day, but in summer they are above ground only in the early morning before the desert sun is high. They hibernate from October until March, often in the same burrow they use for shelter during the rest of the year.

The most notable tortoise adaptation for desert survival is its ability to go for long periods of time without drinking water or eating succulent vegetation. Part of this ability stems from the impervious shell that covers most of its body and the dry scaly skin that covers the rest. Unlike its distant relatives, the amphibians, which lose water continuously through their moist skins, the tortoise loses essentially no water in this manner.

A tortoise has a large water-storage bladder which holds a reserve supply of a pint or more, sufficient to last an entire season. Although they can survive entirely on water from succulent vegetation upon which they feed, tortoises will drink like thirsty camels when water is available. One tortoise was reported to have a 40 percent increase in body weight after a prolonged drink.

During the mating season, male tortoises indulge in vigorous jousting battles in which the object is to turn an opponent over on its back. Given time, a flipped-over male usually can right himself, but if caught in this helpless condition in intense sunlight, may die from the heat.

During copulation, the male is aided in mounting the female by a concave surface in his plastron that matches the convex shape of her carapace. His longer tail helps brace him in a partially upright position. Fertilization is internal, as with all reptiles, and some time after mating the female will lay two to six eggs about the size, color, and shape of golf balls. They are laid in a hole and buried and will hatch in varying lengths of time depending upon the temperature.

For the first three years of their lives, turtles have soft shells and make a very tasty morsel for any predator lucky enough to find them. After the third year, the shells harden and they have fewer enemies to contend with — however, mortality still is relatively high.

In the past, one of the major causes for the population decline of Desert Tortoises was their popularity as pets. It has been estimated that more tortoises exist in the backyards of Los Angeles than in the Mojave Desert. They now are completely protected by law and anyone molesting or

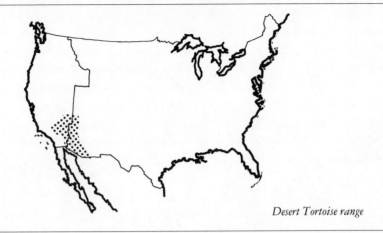

Desert Tortoise range

removing one from its native habitat is subject to a large fine and imprisonment.

Now one of the most potent threats to the future of the Desert Tortoise as well as the fragile desert ecosystem in which it lives, is the proliferation of the "awful ORVs" — the off-road-vehicles. Motorcycles, jeeps, four-wheel-drive trucks, and dune buggies are chewing up the desert at an alarming rate and the Bureau of Land Management, which has responsibility for most of our desert lands, seems to lack both the manpower and the desire to halt this abuse.

When 2,000 dirt bikes line up abreast and roar across the desert from Barstow to Las Vegas, as has happened, fragile desert vegetation that took many years to grow in that harsh climate, is destroyed in one deadly attack. And any unfortunate desert animal, such as the tortoise, that gets in the way of these fun-loving vandals meets the same fate.

Part Three

A NATURALIST'S NOTES

The Black-crowned Night Heron has a scientific
name which means nocturnal crow.

36

Why and How We Use Those
Latin Labels: I've always found it inter-

esting to learn the scientific as well as the common name for plants and
animals I observe and photograph. Many naturalists share this interest in
the technical nomenclature of life forms, but others are completley turned
off at the mere thought of memorizing those long two-part names. They
are seemingly meaningless and, in some cases, virtually unpronounceable.

For example, one might ask why it is necessary to learn to say or spell
Camplyorhynchus brunneicapillus, when Cactus Wren describes the same
bird? Or, why not just say Scrub Jay, instead of *Aphelocoma coerulescens*?

For answers, we need only thumb through field guides to plants or
animals of two regions of the world that have a number of species in
common. For instance, I have before me a copy of a field guide to the birds
of North America and one for Europe.

Opening the European guide, I find a familiar-looking bird labeled the
Goosander, which North American birders know as the Common
Merganser. A glance at the scientific name, *Mergus merganser*, tells me I'm
dealing with the same species, even though it is known by two very
different common names and has populations separated by 3,000 miles of
ocean.

Looking further through the European guide, I encounter a familiar
name under the picture of a very unfamiliar bird. The name is "Robin"
but, despite a red upper breast, it looks unlike any robin I have ever seen.
Checking the scientific name, I discover the European Robin is designated

Erithacus rubecula, not *Turdus migratorius* given for the American Robin in the North American guide. Obviously these are different species, despite having the same common name.

I've also wondered, as I expect many people have, how birds fly, sometimes on very delicate wings. And I've been amazed at the structure of bird's nests. These questions aren't exclusive to any bird or animal so I have added a section that discusses them.

Why and How Organisms Are Classified

When we consider that the animal kingdom alone contains upwards of one million different species, it becomes obvious that some sort of systematic cataloging system is needed to prevent complete chaos. The field of science that deals with this system is known as Taxonomy or Systematics.

The modern system of classifying animals and plants was the brainchild of a 16th century Swedish naturalist, Karl von Linné, who died in 1778. Linné wrote his work in Latin and became famous under the Latinized version of his name, Carolus Linnaeus. Although he was an early pioneer in the field of biological classification, later scientists have been virtually unable to improve on his basic system.

Linnaeus founded what is now known as the "binomial system of scientific nomenclature." In this very formalized system, each distinct type (species) of living organism is given a two-part Latin or Latinized scientific name. The rules are outlined in the International Code of Zoological Nomenclature.

The first part of the scientific name, which is always capitalized, is known as the generic name. The second part, which is never capitalized, is the trivial name. Together, the two parts of the name tell us the species of the organism.

Organisms are cataloged according to phylogenetic (evolutionary) relationships. The "taxonomic hierarchy" consists of seven main categories or "taxons," starting with the most general and ending with the most specific, the species. In order of descending size, these are: Kingdom, Phylum, Class, Order, Family, Genus, and Species.

Taking as an example a species with which we are all familiar, our own, let us consider the way in which it is classified and cataloged by taxonomists.

To begin with, the human species is placed in the broad general category of the animal kingdom or Kingdom *Animalia*. (Some taxonomists consider only two kingdoms, *Planta* and *Animalia*. Others include a third,

158

Kingdom *Protista*, into which are thrown all those organisms, such as fungi and bacteria, which don't fit nicely into either of the other two).

In descending order, the next category in which we find ourselves is Phylum *Chordata*. This large taxon includes all those animals which have a flexible rod of cells called a notochord during their embryonic development. Chordates range from animals as primitive as Marine Acorn Worms to forms as advanced as humans and whales.

Phylum *Chordata* is further subdivided into a number of classes. Humans are in Class *Mammalia*, the mammals. Although mammals may differ greatly in size and general appearance, they all share certain characteristics: They are warm-blooded, air-breathing, hairy skinned (even whales have a few hairs), and they suckle their young from milk-secreting glands. A few very primitive mammals lay eggs but most give birth to living young.

As there are over 8,000 living species of mammals, it is necessary to further subdivide this taxon. The next lower category is order and humans are in Order *Primates*. All primates share two organs of special development; A large and complicated brain and a supple hand with an opposable thumb.

Humans are placed in Family *Hominidae*. This is known as a monotypic family, for it contains only one living species (ignoring the possibility that a bigfoot-type creature exists). Other primate families include *Pongidae*, the anthropoid or man-like apes; *Cercopithecidae*, the Old World monkeys; *Callithricidae*, the marmosets and tamarins; *Cebidae*, the New World monkeys; and several others, such as the lemurs in Family *Lemuridae*.

Humans are in Genus *Homo*. This is a monotypic genus, for it contains only a single living species. Scientists have identified and classified fossil humans that are considered to be in Genus *Homo* but of a species different from our own.

The species of all existing humans is *Homo sapiens*. Our species has been further subdivided into various races or geographical variations.

To summarize, the complete taxonomic classification of our own species is:

> Kingdom — Animalia
> Phylum — Chordata
> Class — Mammalia
> Order — Primates
> Family — Hominidae
> Genus — *Homo*
> Species — *Homo sapiens*

The tiny hummingbird's wings are almost entirely hands.

37

H ow Birds Fly: That birds can fly
is pretty well taken for granted, and few
of us ponder how they are able to accomplish this amazing feat. The truth
is that birds fly in very much the same way as airplanes, and obey the laws
of aerodynamics that aeronautical engineers must consider when designing
aircraft.

The three basic requirements for powered flight are wings, a propeller,
and an engine to drive the propeller. As the designers of the huge C5A
have shown us, any object, regardless of how heavy or awkward in shape,
can be made to fly if there is a big enough wing of proper shape to lift it
and enough energy to drive it through the air. Propellers, of course, don't
have to be in the form of rotating fan blades, but can be of any design that
provides sufficient propulsive or thrust force.

During some 140 million years of evolution, birds have combined the
lifting surface and the thrusting force in a single pair of appendages,
replacing the almost useless forelimbs of their bipedal reptilian ancestors.
These modified forelimbs vary greatly among the 8,600 living bird
species, depending upon what style of flight (or nonflight in some cases) is
best suited for the particular ecological niche of each.

In man's early attempts at powered flight, he foolishly tried to emulate
birds without first understanding what was going on. If a bird could fly by
simply flapping its wings, why couldn't man strap on a pair and do the
same thing? Many tried, but few tower divers ever got a second chance to
modify their equipment or improve their techniques.

It wasn't until the development of high-speed movie cameras that we really began to understand the complex movements in the flapping of a bird's wings. Far from being just a simple up and down movement, the powered and soaring flight of birds involves precise and independent movements of even individual feathers in the hand portions of the wings.

Birds obtain the lift that keeps them airborne from the differential pressure of air passing over the upper and lower surfaces of the inboard or arm portion of their wings. This lift occurs whether the bird is flapping its wings or not, as is demonstrated by soaring birds that remain aloft for hours with scarcely a beat of their wings. The energy that keeps them up is provided by thermal updrafts or wind deflected upward by hills and ridges.

The forward thrust needed to keep air flowing fast enough over the lift portion of the wings is provided, in nonsoaring flight, by the complex propeller action of the primary flight feathers in the hand portion of each wing. The flapping of the rest of the wing simply produces greater effectiveness of the hand portion by moving it faster and through a greater arc.

We can learn a lot about a particular birds' flight style by studying the shape of its wings and the relative size of its arm and hand portions. At one extreme are the tiny hummingbirds that never soar or glide and have wings that are almost entirely hand. The elbow and wrist joints of hummingbirds are practically rigid, and their entire wings function as a pair of variable-pitch propellers that beat so fast they cannot be seen. Only hummingbirds and helicopters are able to fly backwards.

At the other extreme are the world's greatest masters of the art of dynamic soaring, the albatrosses. Their short hand-wings have the usual 10 primary flight feathers found in other birds, but their arm wings are so long they accomodate 40 or more secondary flight-feathers, compared to the 6 to 12 for most other birds. The largest of these birds, the wandering albatross, has wings that span 11½ feet (3.5 meters) but are only 9 inches (23 centimeters) from front to back. The wandering albatross may circumnavigate the globe several times each year and often stays at sea for months or years without setting foot on land.

The majority of birds fall between hummingbirds and albatrosses — having a more equitable balance between arm and hand wings, and flying by various combinations of flapping and gliding. Wing shape is directly related to speed — those birds with broad, rounded wings are slower than those with narrow, pointed wings.

Soaring birds of prey have broad wings with open slits between the primary feathers at the tips that allow them to glide for hours with very little expenditure of energy. These same high-lift wings can be partially folded to form a high-speed low-drag profile, enabling birds such as the Golden Eagle to exceed 100 miles (161 kilometers) per hour when stooping on prey.

Man's greatest shortcoming in attempting the self-powered flight of birds was his puny engine. The pectoral or chest muscles of man are but a tiny fraction of his weight, while those of birds typically range from 15 to 25 percent of body weight — 30 percent in hummingbirds. A hummingbird hovering at a trumpet vine is burning energy about 10 times as fast, in relation to its body weight, as a human running nine miles per hour. If a hummingbird weighed as much as an average human male, it would expend an unbelievable 155,000 calories during a normal day's activities.

Did you ever wonder why the breast meat of quail, pheasant, chicken and turkey is white while that of geese and ducks is red? The type of muscle used to power a bird's wings depends upon its mode of flight. Geese and ducks are long-distance fliers and must expend energy for hours on end without fatigue. Their breast muscles are heavily supplied with blood to provide oxygen and carry off waste products.

The white-meated birds can fly rapidly for a short distance but quickly tire and must return to earth to rest. None are migrants — they simply can't fly far enough without resting. Their typical flight pattern, when fleeing danger, is to climb quickly with a rapid beating of their short wings, and then to glide to safety with a quick loss of the elevation they so laboriously gained.

Each species of bird has a characteristic way of flapping its wings, which can be used by astute birders to identify them at very long distances. In general, wing-beat rate is directly related to size, the smaller the bird, the quicker it flaps. A hummingbird beats its wings about 60 times per second, a chickadee 27, a mockingbird 14, and a domestic pigeon about 3.

Some birds, such as the Red-shouldered Hawk, fly by a combination of several wing beats followed by a short glide. Others, like woodpeckers, undulate in flight by alternating between rapid and slow wing beats. All birds can increase their normal wing-beat rate when flying faster to escape danger.

The Horned Grebe builds a water-bed nest.

38

Birds as Architects: I am amazed by the number of bird nests that appear after leaf fall each autumn. These same nests were so difficult to find in spring, when their owners built them in the shelter of leaf-covered boughs. Almost every roadside deciduous tree will have several nests — they stand out against the stark gray skies of winter, long after the avian engineers that constructed them have migrated.

It would seem a difficult task to identify the builders by these weathered cups of twigs and grass, but observant naturalists can often tell exactly who the departed owner was. Important clues are size, shape, materials used, whether in a tree or on the ground, and type of tree or shrub. Each species has an instinctive behavior pattern for nest building (or nonbuilding in some cases), instincts passed on from generation to generation by means of microscopic chromosomes in the nucleus of egg and sperm.

That nest building is an innate rather than a learned behavior is obvious. Consider the fact that a young bird, nesting for the first time in its second spring of life, will have had no opportunity to watch construction of a nest by its own kind. Yet, the first time a Bullock's Oriole is a parent, it will know exactly how to strip the bark from a willow shoot and weave it into the beautifully designed hanging cup that is characteristic of this species.

Bird nests come in almost as many different forms as do the living creatures that build them. Some birds are lazy — if we can attribute this human trait to the nonhuman world — and build no nests at all. The moth-like Poor-Will simply lays its two white eggs on bare ground, often under the overhang of a sheltering rock outcrop. The Killdeer, one of our most common ground nesters in the West, scrapes out a slight depression in gravely soil and lays its four spotted eggs.

Many birds are underground nesters and either dig burrows or use the tunnels of other burrowing animals. The Belted Kingfisher digs a tunnel as much as 15 feet (5 meters) into a steep-cut stream bank and lays its clutch of five to eight white eggs in an enlarged chamber at the end. The little Burrowing Owl takes over the unused burrow of a California Ground Squirrel, both as a spring nest and as a shelter at other times of the year.

Some ground-nesting birds build elaborate grassy cups with an overhead roof to protect the eggs and young from the elements and to shield them from the eyes of hungry predators. The Western Meadowlark builds a roofed-over tunnel leading up to its beautifully constructed nest of grasses. The nests are so well concealed that some bird watchers have searched in vain in a 20-foot (6-meter) diameter patch of grass where they knew one was hidden.

Many of our larger birds of prey build large stick platform nests that are added to each nesting season until they assume magnificent proportions. Bald Eagle aeries reach 10 feet (3 meters) in diameter and 20 feet (6 meters) in depth and may contain tons of material.

Raptorial birds must enjoy having houseplants, for many hawks and eagles top their nests off with one leafy green bough that is changed for a fresh one as it withers.

Water beds may be relatively new to humankind, but not to birds. The highly aquatic grebes, members of one of the most primitive of bird orders, have built floating nests for millions of years. This technique has restricted them to nesting in quiet, shallow water, where emergent vegetation provides anchors to prevent the nests from floating away. The comical coots, which are only remotely related to grebes, build similar floating nests. However, coot nests are better constructed and their eggs, which are less cold-hardy than those of grebes, remain above the water. Grebe eggs seem to be continually wet, but hatch anyway.

Higher up in the same copse of cattails that may conceal a grebe or coot nest, one may find the beautifully woven cup of a Yellow-headed Blackbird or the globe-shaped home of the Long-billed Marsh Wren. By weaving several cattail leaves together to support their nests, these avian architects take advantage of the engineering principle of resiliency — the ability to be bent without breaking and to return to the original shape when the force is removed. Cattails are seldom broken off by wind.

There always seem to be far more Long-billed Marsh Wren nests in a given area than there are birds to occupy them. This is due to the hard-working male's habit of building up to 10 unlined dummy nests in his territory before the female arrives on the scene. Never satisfied with his inept attempts, however, this liberated female builds the actual brood nest herself.

Hanging nests, such as those built by the brilliant Bullock's Oriole, are among the most beautifully constructed of avian nurseries. The tiny 3½-inch (9-centimeter) Common Bushtit builds a gigantic pendulous nest that may hang as much as 18 inches (46 centimeters) below its attachment to the fork of a small branch. As many as 15 tiny white eggs have been counted in these sock-like nests. The entrance is near the top and the brood-chamber is in the toe end.

Learning to identify bird's nests can be an exciting pastime that adds another dimension to birding. Active nests are most easily located by observing the behavior of adult birds. Carrying of nesting material or food is a dead giveaway, although most birds will not go to the nest if they suspect they are being watched.

Care should be taken to minimize disturbance of nesting birds. Some of the shier species may abandon a nest if there is too much human activity in the area.

When photographing a nest and its occupants, never clip off any foliage around it to obtain a clearer view. This may expose the eggs or young to the heat of the sun or allow them to be more easily seen by predators. Instead, carefully tie back the intruding branches while making a few quick exposures and then return them as nearly as possible to their original positions.

[BIBLIOGRAPHY]

Bakker, E. *An Island Called California* — an ecological introduction to its natural communities. University of California Press; 1972.

Borror, D.J. and R.E. White. *A Field Guide to the Insects of America North of Mexico.* Houghton Mifflin Co.; 1970.

Burt, W.H. *A Field Guide to the Mammals.* Houghton Mifflin Co.; 1952.

Cahalane, V.H. *Mammals of North America.* The MacMillan Co.; 1961.

Levi, H.W., et. al. *Spiders and Their Kin.* Golden Press; 1968.

Murie, O. *A Field Guide to Animal Tracks.* Houghton Mifflin Co.; 1954.

Palmer, E.L. and J.S. Fowler. *Fieldbook of Natural History.* McGraw-Hill Book Co.; 1975.

Peterson, R.T. *A Field Guide to Western Birds.* Houghton Mifflin Co.; 1941.

Robbins, C.S. et.al. *Birds of North America – A Guide to Field Identification.* Golden Press; 1966.

Small, A. *The Birds of California.* Collier Books; 1974.

Stebbins, R.C. *A Field Guide to Western Reptiles and Amphibians.* Houghton Mifflin Co.; 1966.

Storer, T.I. and R.L. Usinger. *Sierra Nevada Natural History.* University of California Press; 1963.

Swan, L.A. and C.S. Papp. *Common Insects of North America.* Harper and Row; 1977.

Tyler, H.A. and D. Phillips. *Owls By Day and Night.* Naturegraph Publishers, Inc.; 1972.

Udvardy, M.D.F. *The Audubon Society Field Guide to North American Birds, Western Region.* Alfred A. Knopf; 1977.